SENSATIONAL
SCRAP QUILTS

By Darra Duffy Williamson

American Quilter's Society
P. O. Box 3290 • Paducah, KY 42002-3290

Library of Congress Cataloging-in-Publication Data

Williamson, Darra Duffy.
Sensational scrap quilts / by Darra Duffy Williamson
p. cm.
Includes bibliographical references.
ISBN 0-89145-983-9: $24.95
1. Patchwork--Patterns. 2. Quilting. I. Title. II. Title: Scrap quilts.
TT835.W535 1992   91-46140
746.9'7--dc20   CIP

Additional copies of this book maybe ordered from:

American Quilter's Society
P.O. Box 3290
Paducah, KY 42002-3290

@$24.95 Add $1.00 for postage & handling.

Title Page Photograph:
DASHING FOR DARRA, 80" x 94",
Sarah Porreca, Hillsborough, NC, 1990.

WINTER STAR, 50" x 50", by the author, 1989. A combination of
two traditional 16-patch blocks. Collection of Carley Anne Morreale.

DEDICATION

To Bobby...
you are, indeed,
"my lucky star"

ACKNOWLEDGMENTS

Although I am the one who sat at the word processor and pushed the keys, this book would not have been possible without the cooperation, assistance and support of many others.

First, and foremost, I would like to thank the talented quiltmakers who so willingly shared their work. Some are former students, some are fellow teachers and colleagues, some just talented women whom I have had the good fortune to know. Happily, all are friends: Nina M. Baker, Marietta E. Breidenthal, Lauralyn Tassin Chapman, Darlene C. Christopherson, Martie Culp, Patricia Mullins Gabriel, Kimberly L. Gibson, Priscilla E. Hair, Ruth H. McIver, Sarah E. Porreca, Amparo Robledo, Lois Tornquist Smith, Debbie Steinberg, Bettydeen S. "Bunny" Tassin, Ruth Templeton, Nan Tournier and Mary Underwood.

Thanks, as well, to the following generous individuals who parted with their quilts long enough for them to be photographed: Matthew and Jason Brown, Beryl Eldring, Rosemary Gabriel, Mr. and Mrs. Herbert Todd McIver, Carley Anne Morreale, Karol Schoenbaum, Max Tassin and Shelton E. Wilder.

Special recognition must go as well to:

Photographer Michael Siede of Studio 111, Boone, North Carolina for his talent, patience and sense of humor;

Debbie Steinberg and Mary Underwood for offering emotional support, providing physical labor, meeting ridiculous deadlines...and still being my friends!

Lois Smith for her advice and encouragement;

Anne Hannon, who helped with the proofreading;

Vicki Faoro and the Schroeders of AQS for their faith in this project;

...and my dad, Charles E. Stever, who travels the world enriching my fabric collection, yet has always been there for me.

PHOTO CREDITS

All photographs by Michael Siede, Studio 111, Boone, North Carolina (unless listed below). Cover photographed at the Manor at Green Hill Bed and Breakfast, Valle Crucis, North Carolina.

Photographs by Bobby Williamson:
Page 67, Plate 5-2
Page 70, Plate 5-3
Page 94, Plates 6-11 (a-c)
Page 95, Plate 6-12 and Plate 6-13

TABLE OF CONTENTS

INTRODUCTION

To state it quite simply: I love scrap quilts! I love to see them, to collect them, to sleep under them...but most of all, I love to make them. And although I admire and applaud the new directions today's quiltmakers continue to explore, it is the scrap quilt – old or new – in the nineteenth century tradition that I seem to love the best.

Like many quiltmakers, my very first quilt was a sampler. I learned the basics of quiltmaking on a full-sized quilt, each block different. The challenge of technique was as much as I could handle: this initial effort is white, red, yellow and blue, all but one fabric solids. Mastering my sewing machine, a thimble, grain line and quarter-inch seams left me too drained to tackle mixing printed fabrics as well.

The years have passed. I have changed and my quilts have too. Now it is not at all uncommon for me to include over 100 different fabrics in a wallhanging-sized piece, with not a solid in the bunch. When I share these multifabric quilts in a workshop, students will ask whether I was born with the ability to mix so many fabrics in a single quilt or whether this is a skill that can be learned. I never hesitate to tell about (or show, if possible) my first quilt. That never fails to answer the question!

I frequently travel and teach. Successful, Sensational Scrap Quilts is my most popular and oft-requested workshop. My fascination with and attraction to scrap quilts is one many quilters seem to share.

The goal of this particular workshop is to encourage the quilter to look at her burgeoning fabric collection in a new way, to understand a little better the treasures she has collected and to gain the knowledge (and often the courage!) to use them. As a teacher, it is always a treat to see a quilter break from her usual quilting "mold," to reach for a fabric in a color she would never previously have *dreamed* of using, to cast aside the "rules and regulations" of quilting that seem to multiply daily and to experience the pure joy of discovering her own creativity. I have found the traditional nineteenth century scrap quilt to be the ideal vehicle for stimulating this type of creative growth experience.

The intention of this book is much the same. By reading through from cover to cover, by pausing to study and admire the wonderful quilts pictured here, and then by actually getting out your fabric and experimenting with the method presented, I hope that you will be challenged "by the old" to try something new. Perhaps you will explore a color that varies from your usual preference; perhaps you will cut into that peculiar "bird" fabric you've never thought to use. You may discover that you enjoy "playing" on a design wall or beginning a quilt with no pre-determined plan. There are so many lessons to be learned from those wonderful old scrap quilts: lessons about color and the richness of printed fabric, lessons about design and process, and lessons about creative freedom that few other quilt genres can teach us! I hope that you will use the "workshop" presented here to help unlock these lessons.

A word of warning: This is NOT a book about basic quiltmaking techniques. I shall not attempt to teach you the rudiments of hand and machine piecing, how to perfect your quilting stitch or the finer points of applique. There are many wonderful books already in print that cover these matters thoroughly and efficiently. In fact, you will find a number of them listed in the bibliography at the end of Chapter 10.

What you will find in these pages is a great deal of insight into your particular collection of printed fabric. You'll find guidance – and reassurance – as you explore a design process, lots of tips and tidbits designed to make scrap quilt construction simpler, some good basic drafting information, a smattering of quilt history and the inspiration provided by many beautiful traditional scrap quilts – old and new.

To get the most from this book, I suggest that you read once through the entire text, pausing, of course, to enjoy the wonderful quilts! Then it is time to go to your workspace, surround yourself with fabric, return to page one, roll up your sleeves and get started. I believe that you will learn from – and thoroughly enjoy – the experience. And, in the unlikely event you never make another scrap quilt, I think you will find that your quiltmaking, whatever your style, will have taken on a freshness and freedom you never expected!

CHAPTER 1
The Nineteenth Century Scrap Quilt

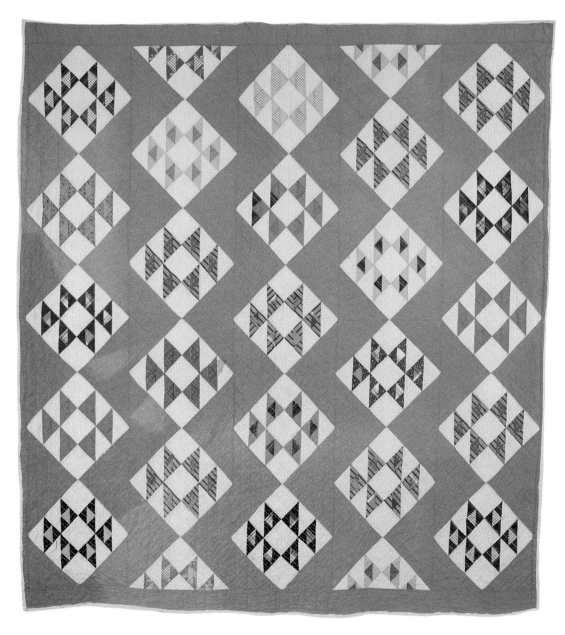

Plate 1-1
HOVERING HAWKS, 70" x 76", Ohio, ca. 1880. Collection of the author. This repeat block quilt (36-patch) makes a striking visual statement with its "bubblegum" pink fabric and exciting set.

THE NINETEENTH CENTURY SCRAP QUILT:
THE TRADITION & THE MYTH

Different Perspectives: Defining The Scrap Quilt

A woman once asked me what type of workshops I teach. When I explained that one of my most popular classes was on scrap quilts, she began to laugh. "You mean you have to TEACH people how to make SCRAP QUILTS!" was all she could manage to say. This woman was born of a generation that had survived especially hard times. Her quiltmaking began as an answer to necessity rather than an inclination, and her home, in a very remote area of our state, made access to store-bought fabric quite difficult. To her, *scrap* quilts are just that: bedcoverings made from the leftovers and remnants of fabric put to other use, constructed in random fashion to take full advantage of the materials at hand. I must admit that when I considered her particular perspective, the idea of purchasing fabric for and actually planning a scrap quilt did seem rather humorous.

Yet for many who have come to quiltmaking in the past decade with little actual home-sewing experience – and therefore no real scrapbag – making a quilt from anything other than purchased yardage is almost equally as foreign. True, quiltmaking itself results in an accumulation of cotton scraps, but by and large, the fabric collections of many of today's quilters consist of quarter, half and full yards of fabric acquired specifically for the purpose of making quilts. Even "scrap" quilts are planned and made from this acquired fabric.

Arriving at a precise definition of a scrap quilt is therefore extremely difficult. Life experience, circumstance, even the quiltmaker's native region can color her perception of this popular quilt genre. In its most general terms, however, I define a scrap quilt as any quilt composed of a multitude of fabrics used somewhat randomly in its composition. The fabric may come from purchase, trade, recycling, "leftovers" or any combination of sources.

The key words in this definition are "multitude" and "randomly." It is impossible to specify a certain number of fabrics as necessary to call a quilt "scrap." A lot depends upon the size and format of the quilt. Most of my scrap quilts involve anywhere from 50 to 250 different fabrics, although I have seen quilts that contain many, many more. By random placement of fabric, I simply mean that you will not find the same fabrics in the same combinations repeated consistently throughout the quilt.

If you are still uncertain as to what exactly constitutes a scrap quilt, you need only glance through the pages of this book – even this chapter – to see many excellent examples. Some have a different combination of fabrics in every block (plate 1-2). In others, the quiltmaker relies on one particular fabric to unify the blocks (plate 1-3). In still others, every single *piece* is cut from a different fabric (plate 1-4)! Yet all somehow fit the definition – both by word and to the eye – of a scrap quilt.

A Brief Overview: Scrap Quilt History

Despite a prevailing myth that the quilt is a purely American invention, both patchwork (pieced and appliqued) and quilting easily pre-date the landing of the Pilgrims at Plymouth Rock. In fact, evidence exists to place these forms of needlework well back into ancient times.

Although our American forebears did not invent quilting, they did embrace it wholeheartedly, quickly imbuing it with a style uniquely their own. While many early examples demonstrate the medallion style so popular in the Old World, by mid-nineteenth century, the overall (or repeat) pieced block format had emerged and flowered, a style Jonathan Holstein refers to as "quintessentially American."[1]

The use of remnant fabric for all or part of a quilt is evident in this country's quiltworks as far back as the late 1700's. Expensive imported fabric was cut to provide large central motifs for *broderie perse* (chintz) applique. Precious leftovers could then be pieced to form borders for these medallion designs. Some of the earliest examples of *pure* block style also date to the eighteenth century and involve pieced and reassembled linsey-woolseys.[2]

A number of factors in the mid-nineteenth century contributed greatly to the rise of the multifabric, block-style quilt in America. By 1840, the textile industry in this country was past its infancy and producing commercial fabric in large quantities. Quiltmakers were no longer dependent on expensive imports or their own home labors to produce the raw materials necessary for their quiltmaking. As fabric became more accessible and less

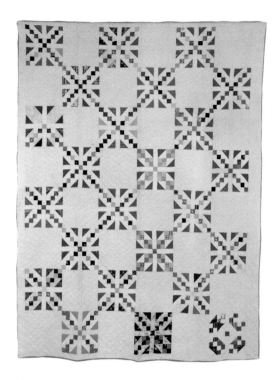

Plate 1-2
COUNTRY CROSSROADS, 70" x 92", Tennessee Valley, ca. 1880. Collection of the author. Each block in this charming quilt is pieced from a different combination of fabrics.

Plate 1-3
GRANDMOTHER'S FLOWER GARDEN, 61" x 80",
Western North Carolina, ca. 1925.
Muslin pathways and consistent yellow centers
bring order to this diverse fabric garden.
Collection of the author (one-patch: hexagon).

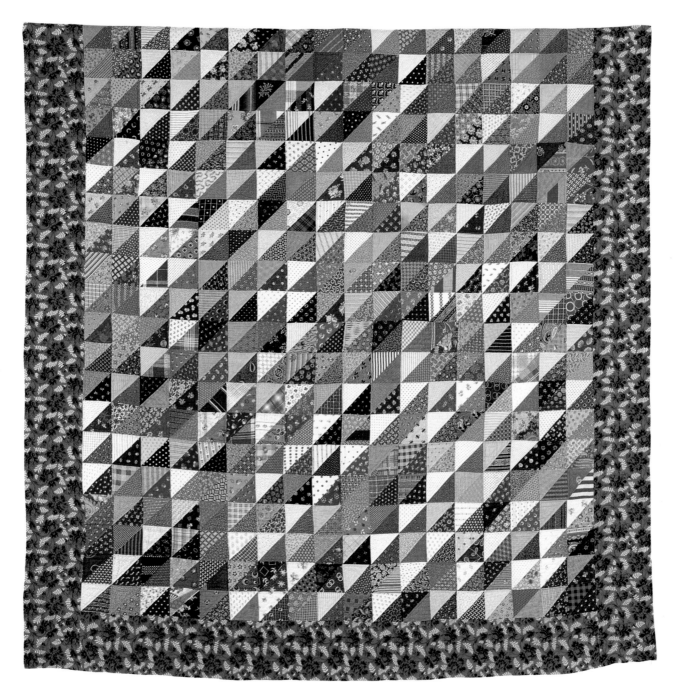

Plate 1-4
TRIANGLES, 80" x 80", Pennsylvania, ca. 1875.
Collection of the author. A true charm quilt,
with each of its 720 right angle triangles cut
from a different fabric. In pristine condition,
this quilt has seen little use and has never been
washed (one-patch: right angle triangle).

expensive, experimentation became viable. The chintz medallion style of quiltmaking began to pass from favor.

With the discovery of the first aniline dyes by William Henry Perkins in 1856, confidence grew in the colorfastness of commercial fabric. Dazzling new colors appeared and the quiltmaker's palette increased. By mid-century, the variety of fabrics was staggering. Chintz, woodblock prints, calicos, pinstripes and rainbow prints were all available for use in clothing or in home decor.[3] Many of these fabrics eventually found their way into quilts, either directly from the dry goods shelf or later, via the scrapbag. The development of the roller printing method, which peaked around 1876, not only produced massive quantities of fabric both colorfast and inexpensive, but also allowed for design detail previously unattainable – or inconsistent at best.[4]

Simultaneous to the boom in the domestic fabric industry was the development of the sewing machine. Originally patented by Elias Howe in 1846, the sewing machine was refined, then widely – and cleverly – marketed by Isaac Singer in the 1850's and 1860's. By 1870, it had become a fixture in many American homes. Is it any wonder that the appearance of the sewing machine, coupled with the dramatically increased availability of commercially manufactured fabric, should lead to an explosion of pieced quilts in this country in the mid-nineteenth century? So great was the explosion, in fact, that quilt historian Barbara Brackman attributes many of today's familiar block patterns to the period from 1865 – 1900.[5] Jonathan Holstein, a devoted enthusiast of the pieced quilt, considers this the era when the most interesting and important contributions were made to the American body of quilts.[6]

The pieced quilt survived into the twentieth century – indeed, even flourished – despite a temporary decline in the quality of cotton fabric around the turn of the century. Shortages caused by war and hard economic times did not affect the popularity of the style, and may, in fact have helped enhance it. Newspapers perpetuated interest by continuing to feature quilt patterns and in 1971, a landmark exhibit at New York's Whitney Museum of American Art secured recognition of the pieced quilt as the American classic it was...and continues to be.

Separating The Myth

No other style of quiltmaking seems to evoke more nostalgia than the scrap quilt. Perhaps it is because so many of us hold fond childhood memories of a Dutch Doll or Dresden Plate or Grandmother's Flower Garden pieced by a doting relative from snippets of Grandpa's pajamas or our own school dresses. Even those with no connection to quilts or quiltmaking in their adult experience can – and do – turn sentimental at the sight of a simply pieced scrap quilt, recalling earlier days and simpler times in their now hectic and complex lives. Such pleasant recollections have done much to spur the current quilt revival, increasing awareness of and appreciation for quilts in general, while enticing countless women and men to begin quiltmaking themselves.

On the other hand, this sentimentality surrounding scrap quilts must bear some responsibility for the stubborn myths that persist even in this day of excellent and exhaustive quilt research. How often have you heard stories of colonial women piecing Log Cabin quilts from the scrapbag remnants of family clothing? Can such tales be true? To the casual observer, truth or fiction is not the point: it is the romance of the image that makes the quilt so appealing. As a quiltmaker, however, and one who constantly relies upon the nineteenth century scrap quilt as a source of inspiration, I have become interested in separating fact from myth and in freeing the scrap quilt from its "poor relation" status in the quilt hierarchy. Were scrap quilts, indeed, simply made from leftovers, hastily and rather crudely constructed to be used "to oblivion" and then replaced? Or were they viewed, even by their makers, as a means of artistic outlet, thoughtfully created from fabric collected, purchased, hoarded and reserved for just this use? I think the answer lies somewhere in between.

While research, oral history and common sense support the theory that many, many multifabric, pieced quilts were born of necessity, frugality and convenience, a growing body of evidence and study suggests that this was not always the case.

One myth easily challenged is that of the afore-mentioned colonial woman placidly piecing quilts from the bountiful contents of her scrapbag, a notion highly suspect for an era when fabric was so dear. Most people owned relatively few garments, and the domestic sewing required to produce them took full advantage of materials available, resulting in few leftovers to augment a scrapbag. It wasn't until the proliferation of commercially produced fabric in the nineteenth century that clothing production escalated to a point that resulted in scraps.[7] Whatever quilts were made by our colonial forebears resulted largely from bulk fabric recycled from other sources, home produced or originally intended for the purpose of making bedcovers.

Jonathan Holstein is one quilt collector who has admittedly modified his stance on the relationship between the pieced quilt and the scrapbag. Originally believing them strictly a thrift medium, he began to suspect that more and more of the pieced quilts he examined were made of fabric acquired specifically for quiltmaking. These observations lead him to conclude that many so-called scrap quilts were produced with artistic, rather than frugal intent. In a symposium paper prepared for the 1985 exhibit "In the Heart of Pennsylvania: Nineteenth and Twentieth Century Quiltmaking Tradition," he states:

> "I am delighted to recognize that what I thought years ago was a triumph over necessity turns out instead to have been a triumph of native design genius consciously applied to a desired aesthetic end. In our great block quilts we can see one of the earliest expressions of the modern spirit." [8]

The idea of the pieced quilt originating solely as a response to poverty and scarcity is likewise questioned by Barbara Brackman, who observes: "In truth, the patchwork quilt demands a certain minimum level of affluence and material goods...since patchwork requires a diversity of fabric." [9]

In her book *The Scrap Look*, quiltmaker and collector Jinny Beyer also proposes that not all nineteenth and twentieth century multifabric quilts were made from leftovers. Although she believes that many probably were made from true scraps, she concludes, on the basis of her research and observation, that "equally as many or more...were made from fabrics carefully saved, traded and, yes even *purchased* with specific quilts in mind."[10]

Myron and Patsy Orlofsky, in their celebrated book *Quilts in America*, add weight to this theory, emphasizing that by the middle of the nineteenth century, "materials were bought specifically for the purpose of making a quilt...the housewife was no longer dependent upon the accumulation of scraps."[11]

The abundance of commercially produced fabrics by the middle of the nineteenth century allowed the quiltmaker increased creative freedom in planning her quilts. Rather than leaving her design choices purely to the random chance of the scrapbag, it is probably safe to assume that many a nineteenth century quiltmaker wrestled with the same creative decisions that we do regarding color, pattern and set for her quilts.

Even in the Southern Appalachians, where many native quiltmakers cling with justifiable pride to the "old ways," some have moved beyond the scrapbag to produce their pieced quilts. Geraldine N. Johnson, in an essay exploring the quilting traditions of the Blue Ridge Mountains of Virginia and North Carolina, conducted a series of interviews with area quiltmakers. In so doing, she discovered that in this region, long considered a bastion of grassroots quiltmaking, certain women are considered "fancy" quilters. Unlike their "plain" quilting sisters, who regard quilts as purely utilitarian and often salvage thread as well as fabric, "fancy" quilters rely on purchased materials for their quilts. Some of these quilts are sold to the tourist trade; others are passed with pride to family members.[12]

What conclusions to draw? Only this: that while it is true that many pieced quilts were constructed as utilitarian objects, with little plan from leftover fabric, we must be wary of assuming that this is universally so. TRIANGLES (plate 1-4, page 15) certainly belies the theory. Although a scrap quilt, it plainly was not created for hard use. Cherished by its maker and revered by her descendents, it was used only for special occasions...or perhaps not at all. It has passed into my hands in pristine condition, never washed, its fabrics crisp and new despite 100-plus years. The fact that so many wonderful nineteenth century scrap quilts have survived into this century is testimony that even the "humble" scrap quilt could be created with care and treated with respect.

Plate 1-5a & b
HOVERING HAWKS, 70" x 76", Ohio, ca. 1880.
Collection of the author. A repeat-block quilt
with an exciting set. (Detail below.)

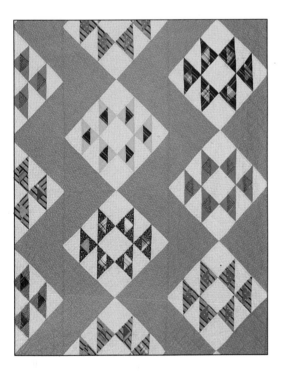

Specific Styles: The Repeat-Block And The One-Patch

While glancing through this book, you will notice that most of the recently made scrap quilts fall into two major design formats: the repeat-block and the one-patch. Each of these styles, firmly rooted in the nineteenth century, is described in the following section. (Note: Although NIGHT SKY, shown on page 109, is an exception, it too can trace its origins to an earlier style – the medallion with its pieced scrap borders.)

An American Classic: The Repeat-Block Style

The overall or repeat-block format involves a single design unit (or block) repeated over the surface of a quilt. The blocks, more often pieced than appliqued, may be set side-by-side, with sashing or plain blocks in between or even turned "on point." (Chapter 7 reviews some of the more common sets for the repeat-block quilt.) Many of the quilts included in this book are repeat-block quilts. HOVERING HAWKS (plates 1-5a & b) and OCEAN WAVES (plate 1-6, page 21) are examples, as are DASHING FOR DARRA in Chapter 2, page 27, LEFTOVERS in Chapter 3, page 35, JAMMED SPOOLS in Chapter 4, page 51, and so on. Look through the text and see how many other examples you can find.

Although the pieced block was in evidence by the post-Revolutionary eighteenth century, its appearance was largely as a secondary design element, frequently framing an appliqued medallion, or alternating with plain strips in a "strippie" or bar quilt (see Chapter 7). It wasn't until the nineteenth century that the *repeat-block* style came into its own and, during the period from 1850 to 1900, achieved a social acceptance not previously realized. The fact that even the majority of fine applique quilts moved from medallion to block format by mid-century indicates the universal recognition the style had received.[13]

Many of the earliest pieced quilt blocks were quite simple in design: Variable Star, Pinwheel, Broken Dishes, LeMoyne (or Lemon) Star. As the repeat pieced block style became more popular, the patterns became more complex, with designs like New York Beauty and Feathered Star challenging the mid-nineteenth century needlewoman. (One notable exception is the Mariner's Compass, which despite its intricacy is regarded as one of

Plate 1-6
OCEAN WAVES, 78" x 78", Pennsylvania, ca. 1890.
The uninhibited use of yellow is a hallmark of the
nineteenth century Pennsylvania quilt. Collection
of the author.

the oldest of pieced patterns.)

Various vogues in quiltmaking probably did much to advance the cause of the repeat pieced block quilt. The popular friendship quilts of the 1840's and the fund-raisers of the later nineteenth century used pieced blocks to record names and information. Lenice Ingram Bacon, in her book *American Patchwork Quilts*, even references Victorian "mourning," "widow's" or "memory wreath" quilts, whose blocks utilized pieces from the clothing of the deceased.[14]

"Fashion" aside, it is easy to see why the repeat-block quilt held such appeal. The ability to construct a quilt top in piecemeal fashion could only be an advantage to quiltmakers working in the confined living quarters many women experienced in the nineteenth century. Large yardages were not necessary; a repeat-block quilt could utilize small cuts of purchased fabrics as well as a variety of remnants and true scraps saved, or perhaps traded with friends and family members. And finally, the repeat-block quilt, while ultimately resulting in something useful, afforded its maker limitless opportunity for creative self-expression. No wonder the style survived the crazy quilt fad of the late 1800's to remain the most enduring quilt format of the twentieth century.

The Versatile One-Patch

An alternative to the repeat-block, and one popular with quiltmakers favoring the scrap quilt, is the one-patch. Despite its seeming simplicity, the single shape offers immense design potential when cut from a wide variety of fabrics.

One of the most familiar – and popular – of the one-patch shapes is the hexagon. Barbara Brackman refers to hexagon patchwork pieced over paper templates as "the classic British quilt"[15] and in nineteenth century England, the mosaic style was produced in untold numbers. The motif soared in popularity in this country; in fact, the first known quilt pattern published in America was a hexagon design in *Godeys' Lady's Book* (January 1835).[16] Silk versions appeared by mid-century and hexagon quilts were popular as "show quilts" throughout the Victorian era. The interpretation known as Grandmother's Flower Garden (plate 1-3, page 14) acquired immense appeal in the twentieth century, peaking in popularity during the 1920's and 1930's and continuing today as the pattern of choice among many quiltmakers.

Interest in the one-patch quilt, coupled with the Victorian penchant for decorative excess, led to the development of a curious trend in the waning years of the nineteenth century. Quiltmakers became fascinated with quilts containing literally thousands of pieces. Patterns such as the Postage Stamp, with its scrap-cut squares measuring less than one inch, became the rage. Quiltmakers sought to outdo each other in perserverence, resulting in quilts with pieces numbering in the tens of thousands! This trend for mega-pieced quilts continued into the early years of the new century, then temporarily disappeared. It returned briefly in the 1930's and 1940's, most notably in the work of Albert Small and Grace Snyder.

One-Patch Phenomenon: The Charm Quilt

During the last quarter of the nineteenth century, another interesting fad surfaced among quiltmakers. The phenomenon was called the "charm quilt" and appears to be linked to other contemporary collecting crazes such as charm bottles and charm button strings. Each of these fads involved young women amassing large collections of a specific item, each somehow different in style. It was not unusual that this collecting fever spilled into needlework, a universal pastime of women of the era.

The charm quilt is most commonly defined as a quilt composed of hundreds of one-patch shapes, each cut from a *different* fabric. Alternately called "beggar's" or "odd fellows" quilts, the style bears witness to the diversity of fabric available by the latter part of the nineteenth century. Combining donations "begged" from family and friends with the contents of her own scrap bag, the quiltmaker strove to collect a target number of fabric pieces. A goal of 999 seems to recur, linked to romantic tales of finding – or not finding – one's "true love" with the acquisition of the 1000th piece. Many quiltmakers surrendered before attaining this elusive number, still managing to produce quilts of amazing richness and variety, as evidenced by TRIANGLES (plate 1-4, page 15), an excellent example of the charm quilt of the day.

Constructed sometime around the nation's centennial, it contains 720 right angle triangles, each cut from a different fabric.

Charm quilts of the late nineteenth century did not use a white or other solid fabric for unity, a trend that was reversed when the fad was resurrected in the 1920's and 1930's. The charm quilts made during this "revival" period relied heavily on the pastel palette popular at the time, often employed the block rather than the one-patch format, and tended to be much lighter in appearance than their earlier counterparts.

Following this brief spurt of popularity, the style again passed from vogue, only to reappear in the 1980's. Quiltmakers became intrigued not only with collecting the necessary variety of fabrics, but also with the unique design challenge posed by such diversity. It is not surprising, then, that the charm quilt remains popular to this day.

Beginnings...

By now you are probably quite anxious to begin creating a scrap quilt of your own. In doing so, I encourage you to look to the scrap quilts of the nineteenth century for inspiration; these old beauties have much to teach. Their influence is evident in almost every quilt I make, no matter how "traditional" or "contemporary," as well as in the philosophies expressed in my workshops and in this book.

So read, look, experiment, create, and enjoy!

Footnotes

[1]Holstein, Jonathan, "The American Block Quilt," *In the Heart of Pennsylvania: Symposium Papers*, p. 16.

[2]Holstein, Jonathan, *The Pieced Quilt*, p. 31.

[3]van der Hoof, Gail, "Various Aspects of Dating Quilts," *In the Heart of Pennsylvania: Symposium Papers*, p. 79.

[4]Brackman, Barbara, *Clues in the Calico: A Guide to Identifying and Dating Antique Quilts*, p. 25.

[5]Ibid., p. 24.

[6]Holstein, *The Pieced Quilt*, p. 83.

[7]Brackman, op. cit., p. 16.

[8]Holstein, "The American Block Quilt," p. 26.

[9]Brackman, op. cit., p. 16.

[10]Beyer, Jinny, *The Scrap Look*, p. 11.

[11]Orlofsky, Myron and Patsy, *Quilts in America*, p. 58.

[12]Johnson, Geraldine N., "More for Warmth than for Looks: Quilts of the Blue Ridge Mountains," *Pieced by Mother: Symposium Papers*, p. 54.

[13]Holstein, "The American Block Quilt," p. 25.

[14]Bacon, Lenice Ingram, *American Patchwork Quilts*, p. 119.

[15]Brackman, op. cit., p. 99.

[16]Ibid., p. 18.

CHAPTER 2
Selecting A Pattern

Plate 2-1
DASHING FOR DARRA, 80" x 94",
by Sarah Porreca, Hillsborough, NC, 1990.
Based on the traditional Churn Dash block
(nine-patch).

SELECTING A PATTERN: GUIDELINES

Plate 2-2
LITTLE PINWHEELS, 12½" x 12½", Amparo Robledo, Boone, NC, 1990. This diminutive quilt, based on the traditional Pinwheel block (four-patch) demonstrates that a scrap quilt need not be large to be successful.

Plate 2-3
TURTLES, 39" x 39," Kimberly L. Gibson, Charleston, SC, 1991. By the addition of a cleverly appliqued "head" and "tail," Kim has turned the traditional Drunkard's Path (four-patch) into something special.

Repeat-Block Or One-Patch?

The first decision you need to make when beginning your scrap quilt is whether you'd prefer a repeat-block or a one-patch design. It is not necessary at this point to decide how big your quilt will be, or how many blocks (or patches) you will need, or even how your quilt will be set. You simply need to decide whether you are more attracted to and comfortable with a repeat-block or a one-patch format.

How do you decide? Try glancing through the photos in this book, as well as those in other quilt books and magazines. (The bibliography on page 146 might help you here.) Look back at the quilts you've chosen to photograph at the quilt shows you have attended. If you are lucky enough to own older quilts made and passed down by family members or collected from various other sources, spread them out and examine them. Which quilts most appeal to you? Do you seem to favor the visual impact created by hundreds of individual triangles pieced in an overall design? Or are you soothed by the symmetry and order of a block (or grid) repeated over the surface of a quilt?

At this point, it doesn't hurt to assess your own personality and skill as a quiltmaker as well. Are you likely to be stimulated by the challenge of creating "order from chaos" using a single shape and hundreds of different fabrics? Does the "thrill of the hunt" appeal to your sense of adventure? Or might you become bored with the hunt *and* the project, preferring instead the more immediate satisfaction of seeing a quilt top take shape quickly, block-by-block? These are points you might consider when deciding whether the repeat-block or one-patch scrap quilt is for you.

The Repeat-Block Format

If the repeat-block idea appeals to you, the next choice you must make is *which* block to feature in your quilt.

My experience has shown that relatively simple block designs are often the most effective choices for scrap treatment. Four-patch and nine-patch variations, the humble Log Cabin and simple Eight-Pointed Star are often overlooked as lacking in challenge for the more seasoned quiltmaker. Yet these simple blocks offer great potential as multifabric quilts. Uncomplicated in design and

Plate 2-4
STAR LIGHT, STAR BRIGHT, 80" x 100",
Ruth Templeton, Horse Shoe, NC, 1988-90.
This beautiful quilt, based on the traditional
Variable Star (16-patch version), has garnered a
variety of regional awards, including Judge's
and Sponsor's Choice.

Figure 2-1
Possible choices for repeat-block format.

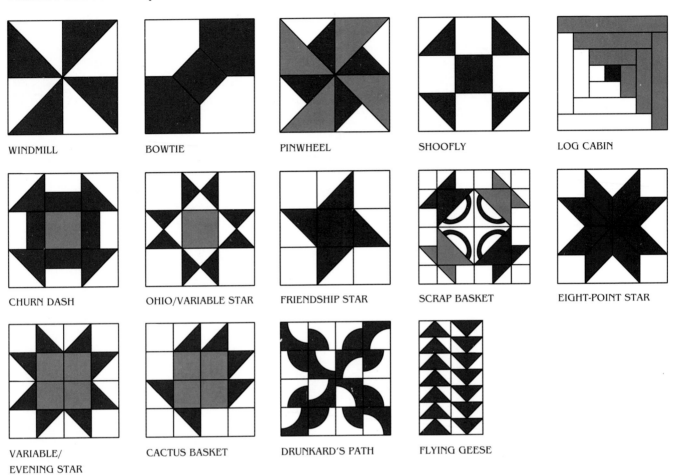

WINDMILL

BOWTIE

PINWHEEL

SHOOFLY

LOG CABIN

CHURN DASH

OHIO/VARIABLE STAR

FRIENDSHIP STAR

SCRAP BASKET

EIGHT-POINT STAR

VARIABLE/
EVENING STAR

CACTUS BASKET

DRUNKARD'S PATH

FLYING GEESE

Figure 2-2
One-patch possibilities.

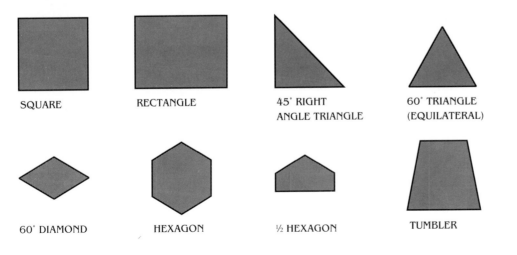

SQUARE

RECTANGLE

45° RIGHT
ANGLE TRIANGLE

60° TRIANGLE
(EQUILATERAL)

60° DIAMOND

HEXAGON

½ HEXAGON

TUMBLER

construction, they let the *fabric* tell the story.

Simplicity, then, is the key word when choosing a block for your scrap quilt. Look for clean, simple lines that will not compete with the busy activity of dozens (or hundreds) of different fabrics. Too many pieces mixed with too many prints can result in a quilt that quickly loses all sense of pattern and design.

Look at the line drawings on the opposite page in figure 2-1. These "old, familiar" blocks are ideal for interpretation in scraps. Each is easy to draft, requires few templates and contains a minimum number of pieces. Almost all are constructed with simple, straight-line sewing, and lend themselves to a variety of quick-cutting and assembly-line stitching methods. Used in a repeat-block format, combining a wide variety of fabrics, each can generate a visual excitement that is hard to match.

The One-Patch Format

If the idea of taking a single shape, cutting it from hundreds of different fabrics and arranging the cut pieces in an overall design sounds appealing, the one-patch scrap quilt may be the perfect choice for you.

You can select a shape as simple as the square or as intriguing as the half-hexagon, depending upon your level of skill or the degree of complexity you desire in your overall design. Figure 2-2 shows a number of one-patch shapes you might consider. Keep in mind that the *colors* you choose to work in, variety in the *visual textures* of the fabrics you select and careful placement of light, medium and dark *values* can yield startlingly different results from the very same shape! We'll explore the possibilities further in chapters to come.

Fabric Collecting: Focus On Charm Quilts

Taking a single shape, cutting it from hundreds of fabrics and still coming up with a pleasing visual whole can be a challenge. But that is part of the fun of the one-patch quilt. Collecting the fabric can be an adventure in itself.

In the first chapter, we introduced the charm quilt, consisting of a one-patch shape, with every piece cut from a different fabric. Not every one-patch quilt is a charm quilt. It is perfectly acceptable to repeat fabrics within a one-patch quilt, just as you would in a repeat-block quilt.

Plate 2-5
MIGRATION, 23" x 30", by the author, 1990.
(Flying Geese, traditional.)

Plate 2-6
TROPICAL REEF, 23" x 23", by the author, 1990.
(Log Cabin/Straight Furrows set). Made for the
Great Art Auction, Watauga County, NC.
Collection of Shelton E. Wilder.

31

Plate 2-7a & b
OCTOBER DAWN, 43" x 33", Priscilla E. Hair, Easley, SC, 1990. This wallhanging, started during a week-long workshop at Cedar Lakes, WV, is based on the traditional Inner City pattern, a divided hexagon one-patch design. (Detail below.)

It's all a matter of personal preference. But for your quilt to be a true charm quilt, *every piece* must be different!

Collecting fabric for any scrap quilt is fun. When making a charm quilt, however, the hunt for variety can be especially educational, social and creative. The following "search strategies" may help enrich your fabric collection for any scrap quilt venture, but are particularly useful should you choose the charm quilt route:

• Try trading through the "swap columns" in popular quilt magazines.

• Organize fabric swaps within your guild and/or small quilting circles.

• Use your guild nametag! Attach a few swatches every time you attend a meeting or seminar and let folks know you're willing to swap.

• Visit garage and estate sales. You might turn up some interesting new "old" pieces to add to your quilt.

• Explore fabric shops that do not necessarily cater to quilters. Check out remnant and sale tables, too.

• Let your family and friends know that you are "on the lookout" and ask them to share their sewing scraps. You may not be able to use all you get, but who knows what treasures you may find? You can donate the excess to schools, senior citizen centers, the church bazaar, etc.

• Gently suggest a few "fat quarters" of fabric as a souvenir from a traveling spouse, family member or friend. (Don't forget to treat *yourself* when *you* are on the road!)

• Check the "quarter yard" baskets at your favorite quilt shops. They frequently contain end cuts, odd pieces, slow movers and golden oldies...unusual fabrics at good prices.

• Offer to bring lunch to a friend if she will let you snip in her sewing room!

Collecting fabrics for a charm quilt can be a long term commitment. This is not the project to undertake if you want a quilt by next month! But quiltmakers who have experimented with the charm quilt often say that making a charm quilt is an engaging experience...in fact, it's hard to stop at one!

Moving On

Once you have decided whether your quilt will be a repeat-block or a one-patch, and you have chosen the block or patch you'd like to try, it's time to explore the design potential of your choice.

Plate 2-8
TURBULENCE, 32" x 27", Mary Underwood, Blowing Rock, NC, 1991. This startlingly original interpretation of the traditional Tumbling Blocks design is actually a charm quilt top. Despite its small dimensions, it contains over 350 different fabrics, cut primarily in the one-patch 60-degree diamond shape. Now completed, this quilt has been a prizewinner many times, including Viewer's Choice at the 1991 Appalachian Quilting Party in Boone, N.C.

CHAPTER 3
Configurations

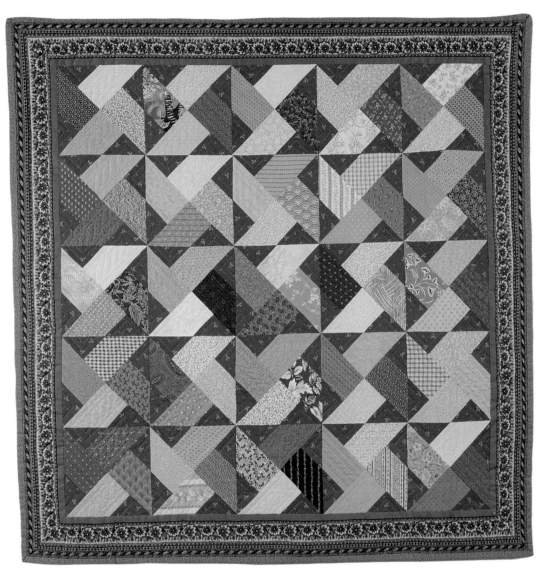

Plate 3-1
LEFTOVERS, 48" x 48", by the author, 1989-90.
Based on the traditional Water Wheel or
Twin Sisters block (four-patch).

CONFIGURATIONS:
THE VALUE OF THE BLACK AND WHITE SKETCH

Defining Value

If there is one mistake quiltmakers seem to make over and over it is in believing that color is what establishes the design or pattern in their quilts. In truth, it is usually not the color, but rather the contrast in *value* that causes the points of the Ohio Star to emerge or the Tumbling Block to appear three-dimensional.

What exactly is value? Value can be most easily defined as the degree of lightness or darkness in color. Quiltmakers most commonly think of fabric in terms of three values: light, medium and dark.

Where you choose to place the light, medium and dark fabrics in a quilt block can have a very dramatic effect on the final appearance of the block. "Scramble", or rearrange the placement of the three values, and a block can take on a totally different personality. Therefore, it is wise – not to mention fun!! – to explore the many possibilities for placing the light, medium and dark values in your block before you begin to cut and sew.

The method that I use for this experiment is a simple one. It frequently leads to at least one or two interesting surprises. Often, it enables me to see a familiar block in an unfamiliar and exciting new way. Occasionally, I save myself considerable disappointment by discovering what I *don't* want to do...and all I have wasted is a few moments of time and a bit of paper.

Try my method. I think you'll like it. But first we must define the term *configuration*.

Configuration: Couldn't Be Easier!!

Don't be intimidated by the word. It's really very simple.

Configuration is the term that I use to describe the appearance of the block once the light, medium and dark values have been assigned their places. A single quilt block can have many different configurations. Each time you rearrange the values within the block, the configuration will change. This offers the quilter a lot of design potential, even for the simplest of blocks. Figure 3-1 shows three possible configurations for the Churn Dash block.

Figure 3-1
Three possible configurations for the Churn Dash block.

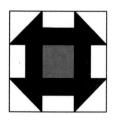 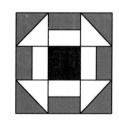 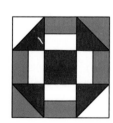

Once you have selected a quilt block that you think might work well for your scrap quilt, you need to determine which configuration of that particular block will work best for you.

Working In Black And White

When you begin to experiment with value in your block, resist the temptation to pull out the colored pencils. Try to do all of your design work in black, gray and white.

There are many advantages to experimenting in black and white as opposed to color. For one thing, it is much easier to differentiate between light, medium and dark when done in absolutes like black, gray and white. Color confuses the issue and colored pencils themselves can be limiting. They rarely, if ever, capture the essence of the printed fabric – or convey its true color when cut and combined with other fabrics.

Working in black and white is also much simpler than designing elaborate fabric mock-ups. Fabric mock-ups can be very time-consuming and can easily lead to a lack of spontaneity. Once a specific piece of fabric has been "committed" to a certain place in your block, it may be hard to make a change later, even if it is for the betterment of your quilt. Glue can be so permanent!

So how do you *visualize* the many configurations a given quilt block might assume? How do you choose which configuration you prefer? What happens when you place together four blocks which use your chosen configuration? And how can you avoid lots of tedious drawing to explore the many possibilities? I use the tracing paper overlay.

The Tracing Paper Overlay: Materials

The materials you will need for your tracing paper overlay include: one sheet of 8½" x 11" graph paper (four squares per inch works best), a few sheets of 8½" x 11" tissue-type tracing paper, transparent tape, ruler and lead pencil or black felt-tipped markers (fine and/or medium point).

"Light" and "dark" values are easy to reproduce. For "dark," press firmly with a pencil or black felt-tipped marker to fill the space completely (BLACK); for "light," leave the space blank (WHITE); for "medium," shade with

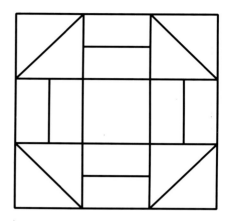

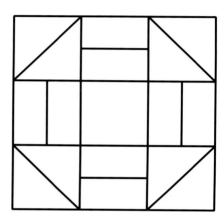

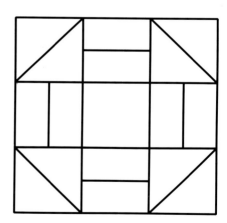

Figure 3-2

a pencil or use the black felt-tipped marker to make dots or slashes (GRAY).

> HINT: The tracing paper will enable you to utilize the same line drawings over and over again and is an easy, inexpensive method for those without ready access to a copy machine.

For Repeat-Block Designs: The Method

Let's experiment! Choose one of the repeat-blocks shown in the previous chapter or any simple block that you think might work well in a repeat-block scrap quilt. Outline the block (figure 3-2) three times on graph paper. *Do not yet color it in!*

- Lay the tracing paper over the graph paper outlines (you can hold it in place with transparent tape) and, using either a lead pencil or black felt-tipped pen, "color" the *first* block, designating dark, medium and light areas with black, gray and white. You now have one configuration of the block.

- "Color" the second and third samples of the block, each time assigning the dark, medium and light values to a new position. Notice how different the same block can look with the values shifted!

- Experiment further. Lift the tracing paper and outline on the graph paper a four-block unit as shown in figure 3-3. Return the tracing paper to position and, choosing one of your newly discovered configurations, use it to color the four-block unit (figure 3-4). How does your block interact with itself? Do secondary designs appear?

- Repeat with a different configuration or try again with another block – one pictured in Chapter 2 or perhaps one of your own personal favorites. REMEMBER: simple often works best.

The design possibilities are endless! Allow yourself time to play (Figure 3-5).

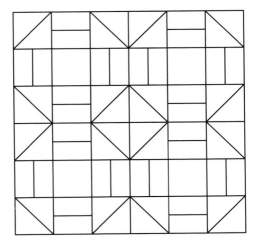

Figure 3-3

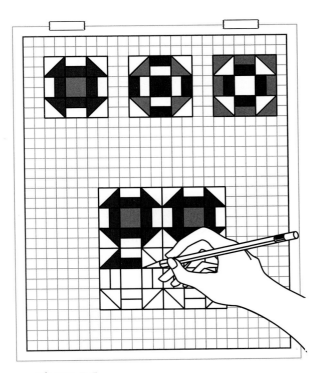

Figure 3-5
Implementing the tracing paper overlay method.

Figure 3-4
Two possible configurations of the Churn Dash block, shown in four-block units.

Plate 3-2
FRATERNAL TWIN II, 57" x 57", by the author, 1989-90. Careful arrangement of light, medium and dark values results in "interlocked" stars which seem to float above a background surface. Based on the traditional Friendship Star block (nine-patch). Collection of Jason Brown.

Figure 3-6
Original black and white sketch for FRATERNAL TWIN II. Light background results in a grid that seems to dominate the design. This configuration was ultimately rejected.

Figure 3-7
The second attempt at a black and white sketch for FRATERNAL TWIN II fails to yield the desired result. Background still dominates.

Figure 3-8
This configuration produces the desired effect: stars appear to "interlock" over a "passive" background.

Theory Into Practice

The quilt FRATERNAL TWIN II (plate 3-2) is a perfect example of how a black and white sketch can preview a finished quilt and avert design disappointment.

FRATERNAL TWIN II is a scrap quilt based on the traditional Friendship Star block. My initial intention was to arrange the light, medium and dark fabrics in such a way as to give the appearance of interlocking stars. I wanted the stars to dominate the design and the background to recede.

When I experimented with three different black and white sketches, I discovered very quickly that only one configuration would give me the effect I wanted. In the first sketch (figure 3-6), I colored the background light and the stars medium and dark. In the second sketch (figure 3-7), the background became dark, with light and medium stars. In both cases, the background grid seemed to dominate the design – not at all the effect I had hoped to achieve.

In my third attempt (figure 3-8), I colored the background squares medium and the stars light and dark. The high contrast between their values caused the stars to "interlock" and the medium value squares seemed to recede into the background, just as I had hoped. This simple experiment on paper saved me lots of wasted time and fabric and resulted in the quilt I had imagined.

The quilt LEFTOVERS (plate 3-1, page 35) provides another good example of the type of discovery that can be made by experimenting with tracing paper overlay. While playing on paper, I found that this block, a traditional pattern called Water Wheel (or Twin Sisters), formed a number of interesting secondary designs when set in a four-block unit. Having discovered this fact before I began cutting fabric, I was able to place my light, medium and dark values to take full advantage of these secondary designs (figure 3-9).

Time To Decide

Eventually the time will come when you need to stop "playing" and make a decision as to which configuration you wish to use in your quilt. You may have no idea of how you want to set your quilt top and whether or not you will take advantage of the secondary designs of a "side-by-

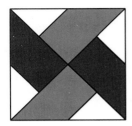

Figure 3-9
Black and white test sketches for LEFTOVERS reveal interesting secondary design potential.

Plate 3-3
TURBULENCE, detail. The 60-degree diamond becomes a block or cube with consistent placement of light, medium and dark valued fabrics. (A full view of this quilt appears on page 33.)

side" set. No matter! I frequently reserve my decision on set until many, if not all, of my blocks are finished. All you need to decide at this point is placement of *value* within the single block. Meanwhile, you have explored your block from many angles and are more aware of some of its design potential. This will come in handy later.

For One-Patch Designs: The Method

You can use the tracing paper overlay method to explore the design potential of the one-patch as well as the repeat-block. Pre-printed graph paper, such as GRAFIX®, which comes in a variety of one-patch shapes, can speed the process.

Some one-patch designs have the value placement determined by the very nature of the block, such as Tumbling Blocks (the 60-degree diamonds arranged in a consistent light, medium and dark cube). Mary Underwood's quilt TURBULENCE, detailed here (plate 3-3), is a good example. But many other variations can be achieved with this and other one-patch shapes by manipulating the placement of dark, medium and light values. Figure 3-10 shows the 60-degree diamond shape arranged in a variety of configurations. By varying the placement of dark, medium and light diamonds, different shapes (hexagons, stars, cubes) dominate.

Now it's time to start thinking about color.

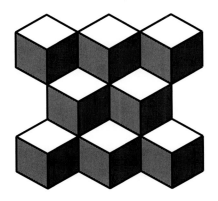

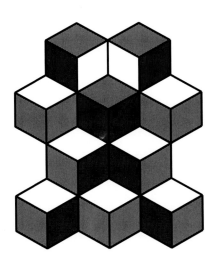

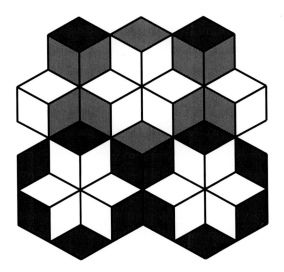

Figure 3-10
Possible configurations for the 60-degree diamond.

CHAPTER 4
Fabric

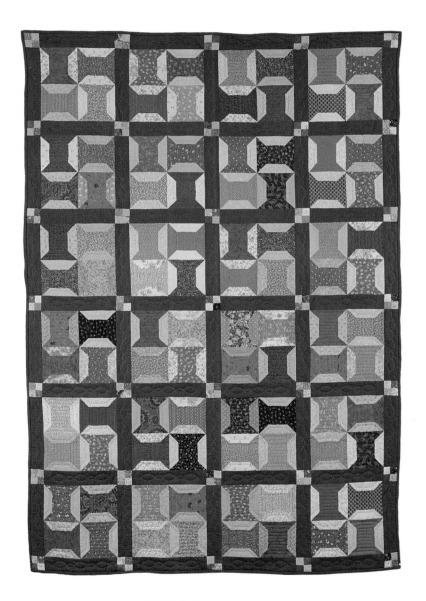

Plate 4-1
JAMMED SPOOLS, 58½" x 88", Nina Baker,
Boone, NC, 1989-90. Based on the traditional
Spools block (four-patch). Nina began with a
color scheme of blue and violet. The addition
of a third color (red), coupled with both liberal
interpretation and careful blending of colors,
resulted in a visually exciting quilt.

FABRIC:
THE "HEART" OF THE MATTER

Fabric! We love it: that is why the majority of us are quiltmakers and not sculptors or watercolorists. Fabric is our medium, a constant source of pleasure and inspiration. And yet, some quiltmakers maintain a curious love-hate relationship with their fabric, considering its acquisition their greatest vice. If you are serious about making scrap quilts – whether from true scraps, purchased fabric or some combination – you will need to overcome any residual shyness you may feel about accumulating fabric. Scrap quilts, by their very nature, require a wide variety of fabrics to be successful.

"Letting Go"

When I first began teaching classes on the scrap quilt, it was not unusual for students to express admiration for the way I handled color – and the wide diversity of fabrics – in my own quilts. Often they arrived armed with photos of luscious scrap quilts from their favorite quilt books and magazines. Antique quilts, shared both through slides and "in the cloth," would elicit enthusiasm and resolve: "I'm in a rut! I want to learn to do that! Teach me to do that!" I heard those words over and over again. Yet, as class progressed, I frequently found the most excited students clinging desperately to the personal (and sometimes limited) "fabric comfort zone" with which they had arrived. Getting these frightened students to "stop fighting and let go" was – and still is – my biggest challenge as a teacher, and one with which I feel I am relatively successful.

Please consider this advice (some students call it my "pep talk") as you begin to make fabric choices for your scrap quilt:

• Look, *really look*, at the scrap quilts you admire. How has the quiltmaker approached the question of color? If you study the nineteenth century scrap quilt, you will probably notice that certain colors tend to dominate: browns, reds, beiges, blacks, mustards, indigos, grays. "Bubblegum" pink and "acid" green are used frequently, particularly in the quilts of the last quarter of the century. Yellow appears – usually in small quantities – to add sparkle. If the nineteenth century look is what you desire, learn the lessons these old beauties have to teach.

If these colors are not particularly to your liking, you

may need to re-think your goals. You might feel more comfortable – and satisfied – creating a scrap quilt in the "style" of the nineteenth century, but in an overall color scheme that is more this century...and "you." Nineteenth century style and twentieth century color sense "marry" well, as evidenced by many of the quilts pictured in this book.

• Stay open-minded! Developing a scrap quilt, with 50 or 100 or even 500 different fabrics, involves a different process – and attitude – than designing a quilt with four or five coordinated pieces. At first some of the colors, fabrics and combinations may seem a bit foreign to you, but it is through experimentation that we discover new things and grow as quiltmakers. Don't begin by limiting yourself with the words: "Oh, I could *never*...." Relax, be daring – and have fun!

Keep in mind that most of the fabrics ultimately used in your scrap quilt will appear in *very small* amounts. The wide variety of fabrics, combined with the small pieces in which they appear, allow you quite a bit of creative freedom. A bright orange, or a rather unusual animal print might seem totally "incorrigible" as a two-yard length, or most inappropriate for your "traditional" quilt. Yet, small pieces can be integrated in such a way as to create interest and add richness. Don't "edit them out" without giving them a chance.

When composing a scrap quilt, it is very important to focus on "the big picture," rather than on every single, individual fabric in the quilt. If you study the details of various quilts pictured throughout this book, you will notice that not every fabric in every block is "pretty." In fact, some of the blocks themselves are not particularly attractive, and yet the overall appearance of each quilt is very pleasing.

Sometimes I think that we overwork the concept of "pretty" when planning our quilts. We worry that every flower in every fabric in every block be "pretty." The end result, unfortunately, is that our quilts run the risk of being pretty...boring!

As you approach your fabrics to begin making choices for your scrap quilt, try to be as liberal as you can. If you choose pink as one of the colors for your scrap quilt, and then pull only the pretty, flowered pinks from your closet, you have already set limitations on your quilt. Remember "the big picture" and pull those "oddballs" as well. They may not all find their way into the finished quilt, but at least you will have considered all your options.

Unlocking the secret to making successful fabric choices for your scrap quilt involves understanding the following "keys": color, visual texture and value. These three key elements are covered in detail as I describe my method for fabric selection. I suggest that you read it through, and then use it as a guide as you begin to choose the fabrics for your own personal scrap masterpiece.

Key #1: Color

When questioned about the area of quiltmaking which leaves them feeling most insecure, many quiltmakers – including some of surprisingly advanced ability – will reply "I wish I were more comfortable about choosing and combining the colors for my quilts." Nothing seems to arouse anxiety in quilters more quickly than the subject of color.

I certainly do not claim to have all the answers! Our preferences, reactions and tolerances for certain colors are highly personal. A color arrangement that seems perfectly acceptable – in fact, downright appealing – to me, might draw a totally contrary response from you. But that diversity is what makes us – and our quilts – so interesting!

What I *can* do, however, is to help you increase your color awareness, easing you into more adventurous color choices for your scrap quilts. If you are feeling a bit inhibited about your ability to work with color, this approach will help to "free you up" to see color in a more expansive way. If, on the other hand, your concern is how to gain some control over a tempting, but seemingly unwieldy spectrum of fabric, this method can assist in creating "order out of chaos." In other words, there is something for everyone.

In addition to suggestions for approaching color, I offer you encouragement. While some people seem to be born with a natural instinct for color, "birthright" is not essential. The ability to deal comfortably with color is a skill that can be learned. I am living proof of that. My first quilt, described in the introduction to this book, was singularly uninspired in the color department. Now, I regard my ability to work successfully and confidently with color as one of my primary talents as a quiltmaker. If I can do it...*so can you!*

Basic Color "Language"

I did not come to quiltmaking with a degree or even much background in art. In fact, the "art" connection to quiltmaking frankly intimidated me. Over time, I have come to realize that part of the problem was that I did not understand the language. Once I became familiar with some basic terminology and a few simple principles, I felt more comfortable reading about, taking classes in and experimenting with color. Perhaps I can help demystify the subject by translating some of these concepts for you.

Hue is just another word for color. A *tint* is a color (or hue) with white added. For example, if you add white to the color orange, peach is the resulting tint. A *shade,* on the other hand, is what results when you add black to a color. Rust, then, is a shade of the color orange.

A *tone* is what you get when you add gray to a color. Think of the "dusty colors" so popular in recent years; these are examples of tones. Many of the fabrics available to quiltmakers over the past ten or fifteen years fall into this category of color. Williamsburg blue, country rose and colonial green all have a very "grayed" look. While these tones are very restful, and wonderful for home decorating, too many of them in a scrap quilt can cause problems – more on that later.

Adding gray lessens the *intensity* of color. The *pure colors* are those that appear on the *color wheel.* They have no gray in them; therefore, they are the most intense.

Remember the color wheel? If you are like me, you achieved a passing acquaintance with it at some point in your education, but never truly grasped what it was all about. Since becoming a quiltmaker, however, I have developed a hearty respect for this helpful tool. While I don't consider it the dictator of my color choices, I find it offers valuable assistance when I'm not certain in which direction to proceed. You may want to refer to a color wheel as you develop the color scheme for your scrap quilt. Since I refer to it later in this chapter, I've included one here for your convenience (plate 4-2).

For a thorough explanation of the color wheel and how

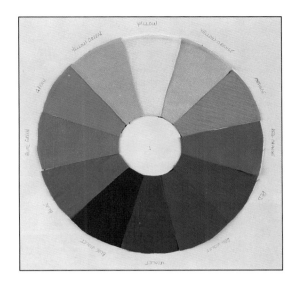

Plate 4-2
Color Wheel.

Plate 4-3
Begin by choosing two colors...
in this case, red and green.

Plate 4-4
Be sure to interpret your colors broadly.
Include pink, brick, burgundy
along wtih true reds.

it works, you may want to check the bibliography at the end of this book. It contains a number of excellent resources devoted solely to the topic of color.

Developing A Color Scheme

Many of us begin our quiltmaking experiences by designing quilts of two colors, in fabrics carefully chosen to coordinate with our own (or the quilt recipient's) home decor. When the desire comes to break out of this two-color, five-fabric coordinated cycle, we are uncertain how to proceed. Scrap quilts, with their seemingly unlimited – and unbridled! – combinations of colors and prints, present a particular challenge. Where and how to begin?

The following method is the one that I use for developing workable color schemes for my scrap quilts. To arrive at it, I read, took classes, relied on instinct...but primarily I studied the scrap quilts of the nineteenth century and heeded the lessons they taught. Then I experimented, and gradually over a period of time, I felt my confidence grow. Here is the method I still use today, when the urge comes upon me to begin a new scrap quilt:

• Begin by choosing a basic scheme of two colors that appeal to you; for example, blue and rust, red and green, blue and burgundy. These can be your two favorites, or two new ones you've never tried before. Select from your collection of fabrics those that "fit" the two-color scheme and arrange them in two separate piles as shown in plate 4-3.

S–T–R–E–T–C–H! Be as liberal as you can be in your interpretation of color. If one of your chosen colors is red, don't overlook the bricks and rusts, the red-tinged browns, the burgundies and the pinks. Consider, and include, all the tints and shades of your two chosen colors (plate 4-4).

Some fabrics may cause difficulty. Perhaps they contain many colors – including your chosen ones – but no particular color seems to dominate. Or perhaps, when viewed from a distance, they appear to be a totally different color, one that doesn't actually appear in the print itself. The important thing at this stage is that you not allow yourself to labor over your decisions. Rely on your instincts. If your initial reaction is to call a fabric "red," do so and add it to the red pile. Don't second guess yourself. Better to be too broad now; you can always eliminate later if necessary.

- Now select a third color. If you are feeling adventurous, you can pick this third color randomly. Or, you might refer to the color wheel and select one of the "neighbors" to a color you have already chosen. Another possibility might be to move directly across the color wheel and select the opposite (or *complement*) of one of your original colors.

  Once you have chosen a third color, return to your fabric collection and pull all of the fabrics that fit this new color. (You might, for example, choose blue.) Remember to be liberal – and don't forget the tints and shades!

- You now have a variety of fabrics before you, in what probably seems an incongruous array of colors. The success of a pleasing scrap quilt will depend a great deal upon your ability to blend these many different colors, with their many tints and shades, into a pleasing visual whole.

  If you have chosen to work along with our red/green/blue example, and have been truly liberal in your interpretation of color, you probably have before you lots of blue fabrics! Some of these blues are probably "true" blue, while many of them have a decidedly blue-green (teal, turquoise) or blue-violet cast. Likewise, you probably have true reds, orange-reds and red-violets (or burgundies), while your greens range from yellow spring greens through greens containing lots of blue. Try to arrange these many fabrics so that the colors blend or flow from one to the next. Give no consideration to the *value* of the fabric – just the *color*. You might begin with the orange-reds, move to true reds, then burgundies (red-violets). From these red-violets, you can move into the most violet of the blues, moving closer to true blue, then blue-green and eventually into the greens. The color wheel can help in determining how to proceed. Plate 4-5 will give you an idea of how this red/green/blue color scheme might blend.

- If you find there are spots where you are having difficulty in "bridging" smoothly from one color into another, resist the urge to start removing fabrics from your color scheme. Instead, refer to the color wheel. Perhaps there is a color that appears *between* the two colors you are

Plate 4-5
Introducing a third color (blue).

Plate 4-6
Detail, JAMMED SPOOLS (full quilt is shown in Plate 4-1, page 45).

Plate 4-7
A few violet fabrics can help reds and blues blend more comfortably.

Plate 4-8
Neutral fabrics can help blend while adding richness to the color scheme.

trying to blend. Return to your fabric collection and add a few pieces in that transition color. In the red/green/blue example, a few shades of plum or eggplant (violets) might help "bridge the gap" from burgundy (red-violet) to blue (plate 4-7). These few new violet fabrics will not result in a purple quilt, but will help your chosen colors blend more comfortably while adding interest to your color scheme. That's what a successful scrap quilt is all about!

· Perhaps you'd prefer not to add additional color to your quilt, but still feel the need to close a few gaps: the *neutral* fabric may be your solution. These beiges and browns, grays and blacks, whites and creams can be added to any color scheme. They will not *change* the basic color scheme, but instead can help unruly colors to coexist comfortably while adding richness and depth to the quilt. Don't be afraid to interpret neutrals broadly – some grays venture naturally into blue; some creams have a decidedly yellow cast (plate 4-8).

· Finally, don't overlook the reverse side of your fabrics. Sometimes there is just enough difference in the back side of a print to supply the subtle color variation you seek.

Wow! The Use Of "Zingers"

If you have achieved a successful flow of color – one that utilizes tints, shades, "bridge" colors and neutrals – you have probably already included two additional elements important to a successful color scheme.

One is the "zinger," sometimes called the "sparkler" or "accent," which can breathe real life into your quilt. Think of it as a brighter, hotter or more intense version of a color already in your plan. In the red/green/blue example we have discussed, the zinger color may be a bright turquoise (blue-green) or a hot pink (a tint of red) or a buttery yellow acting as a neutral. If you *blend* these zingers into your color scheme, they will fit comfortably in your quilt.

Should your color scheme look a bit flat, the zinger may be the missing ingredient. Perhaps you are being too literal in interpreting your chosen colors. Try going back to your fabric collection and approaching your original color scheme with a broader view. Integrate these new, more liberal selections into your scheme and the problem should be solved. If you cannot find any zingers in your fabric collection, you have discovered an important gap. Keep it in mind the next time you go fabric shopping or swapping so this shortage can be remedied.

A word of caution: a touch of zinger goes a long way. In fact, if used with too free a hand, zingers have a way of taking over a quilt, losing their element of visual surprise. So handle them with care – but *do* include them!

Darks For Drama And Depth

The final important ingredient in a successful color scheme is the dark fabric, which can add drama and depth to your quilts. If you have used black, for example, to bridge from violet to navy into blue; or perhaps a wonderful chocolate brown to enrich your reds, you have included the deep, dramatic colors that will give your quilt added dimension (plate 4-10, page 54). Like your zingers, these very dark fabrics should be used with care – too much can make for a somber quilt! Just be sure to include them.

Darkness, of course, is a relative term. If it is your intention to use a palette of light, pastel-type colors, the dark may simply be a deeper, richer shade of one or more of these pastels; for example, a deep mauve or a rich blue. DANCE OF THE SPRITES, Lois Smith's exquisite soft colorwash (plate 4-11, page 55) demonstrates how the concept "dark" is relative to the overall palette of the quilt.

When you are satisfied that your color scheme appeals to your eye, flows smoothly and contains both the lively zingers and the dramatic darks, you are ready to start looking more closely at the "types" of fabrics that you have selected.

Key #2: Visual Texture

There is more to consider than color when examining the large selection of fabrics you have chosen for your scrap quilt. You will also want variety in the visual texture of the fabrics in your quilt.

When we think of "texture" in fabric, certain *types* of fabric usually come to mind: velvet with its soft nap, satin with its slick sheen, corduroy with its ridges. These are all textures that we can *feel* as well as see. They are *tactile textures*.

Plate 4-9
DAWN PATROL, 40" x 40", quilt top by author, 1990. The diagonal nature of the traditional Wild Goose Chase (25-patch) block creates a great deal of motion over the quilt surface. Thoughtful placement of "zinger" fabric helps keep the eye moving.

Plate 4-10
KALEIDOSCOPE, 36" x 48", quilt top in progress,
by Debbie Steinberg, Blowing Rock, NC, 1990-91.
Debbie's original fabric palette for this quilt was
rather subdued. By expanding her interpretation of
color to include both the "zinger" and the dramatic
dark, she has greatly intensified the impact of this
wonderful quilt (eight-pointed star).

Plate 4-11

DANCE OF THE SPRITES, 58" x 68", ©Lois Tornquist Smith, Rockville, MD, 1988. Based on the Pinwheel block (four-patch), this quilt is a wonderful example of Lois's skill as a colorist as well as at her sewing machine. Machine pieced and quilted, it received an Honorable Mention at the 1989 AQS Quilt Show and Contest.

As quiltmakers, many of us confine ourselves to 100% cotton fabric. It is a natural fiber that handles easily, creases nicely, doesn't pill and wears well. All cottons, however, "appear" and "feel" pretty much the same. We must, therefore, rely almost exclusively on the printed design of the fabric to give us the *illusion* of texture. This is called *visual texture.*

When I first began collecting fabric for quiltmaking, I was drawn primarily to pretty, flowery calicos. These tiny, floral prints appealed to my sense of aesthetics. They also represented what I assumed the "traditional" quilt fabric would be and, to a large degree, they were all that was available in 100% cotton. It didn't take me long to realize, however, that a quilt made entirely of "little prints" presented more than a few problems. First of all, many of these little prints contained *lots* of colors, which made them hard to blend together in a quilt. They also tended to be of *medium* value so I found it difficult to achieve any depth or dimension in my blocks. Finally, with all of the prints so similar, I discovered that my quilts were...well, frankly, visually boring!

While I was making my personal discoveries, the fabric manufacturers were making theirs as well. More and more 100% cotton fabrics were becoming available in an incredible range of colors and prints. There is a whole world of choices available to us as quiltmakers today, as long as we are brave enough to venture forward.

To create sensational scrap quilts, you will need a wide variety of visual textures in the fabrics you choose. Examine the fabrics you have selected for your quilt on the basis of color. Among those fabrics, look for:

Figure 4-1
Flowers and florals: in all shapes and sizes, from the tiniest bud to the large cabbage rose .

Figure 4-2
Foliage: from light airy vines to densely packed leaf prints…no flowers.

Figure 4-3
"True" geometrics: checks, plaids, stripes. These are frequently in short supply in a quiltmaker's fabric library, but essential for the development of scrap quilts in the nineteenth century tradition.

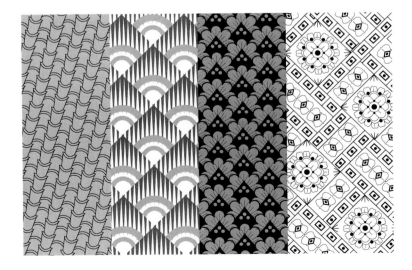

Figure 4-4
"Abstract" geometrics: printed in such a "regular" way as to form a consistent pattern or grid, even though not a true plaid or stripe.

Figure 4-5
Dots and circles: in a variety of sizes.

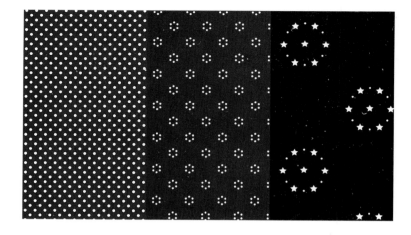

Figure 4-6
"Picture" prints: actual pictures of people, animals or things such as horseshoes, scissors, stars, crescent moons, spools, flags, sailboats. These prints are highly characteristic of the nineteenth century scrap quilt.

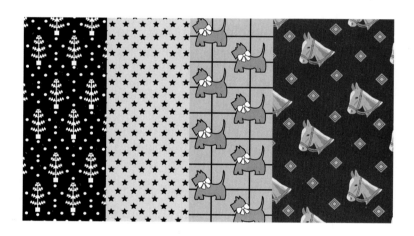

Figure 4-7
"Nature" prints: prints which *suggest* things in nature, such as the sky, water and/or the sea, tree bark, marble, grass.

Figure 4-8
"International" or "ethnic" prints: prints reminiscent of other countries or cultures; for example, those suggesting a Japanese kimono, an African tribal robe, an Indian blanket.

Figure 4-9
Feathers and paisleys: great for introducing large scale pattern.

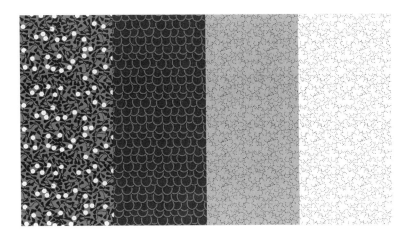

Figure 4-10
"Peaceful" prints: low contrast, read-as-solid and give the eye a place to rest.

Can you find at least a few examples of each in your assembled fabrics? If not, you will want to fill them in. It is the variety of fabrics that will make your scrap quilt appealing. Get the viewer involved in your quilt, with its overall design and color, then "surprise his eyes" as he begins to explore the rich variety of the fabrics themselves.

Key #3: Value

At this point you have selected the fabrics for your quilt, considering both color and visual texture. It is now time to determine their *value* so that they can be properly positioned as you begin constructing your blocks. Remember: the key to the configuration of your block is not which *color* goes where – but which *value*!

When I first began making quilts, I tried to assign fabrics value by sorting them into three piles: light, medium and dark. I quickly became frustrated as I realized that the value of any given fabric is *relative* to the fabrics surrounding it. In other words, a fabric may be light when compared to one fabric and dark when compared to another. Rather than assign each fabric a category which might prove not only limiting, but ultimately incorrect, I found it easier to do a full layout of my fabric on the basis of *value*. In this way, each individual fabric could be judged in relationship to *every other fabric*. I have used this method in one form or another since the earliest days of my quiltmaking career and have found it to be very successful, especially for scrap quilts.

So...take all of the fabrics you have selected for your quilt (on the basis of color and visual texture), mix them up and then try to arrange them, *regardless* of color, from the lightest to the darkest. This will probably prove to be much more challenging than you suspect, and you will learn a great deal about the properties of printed fabric before you are through.

One thing you will quickly discover is that you cannot assign a value to a fabric based solely on its background color. A fabric with a deep blue or a wine or even a black background may prompt you to say, "Well, this is obviously a dark fabric!" But when you place it with the other darks it "jumps" out of place. Why?

When trying to assign each fabric a "value position,"

Plate 4-12
A fabric reference card shows the relative value of every fabric in your chosen color scheme.

you must look at the *whole* fabric and not just the background. A fabric with the deepest black ground, when printed with a profusion of pink roses and pale green leaves, will lose its dark status and perhaps shift down into the medium range.

If you have arranged your fabrics from lightest to darkest, regardless of color, but are still uncertain as to the validity of your arrangement, there are a number of tests that can be applied:

- A *valuefinder* is a helpful tool in determining relative value. This red plastic strip or square can be held in front of your eyes while viewing a run of fabrics. The red helps to filter out the confusing element of color, presenting the fabrics as black, white and gray, making it easier to focus on value and to discover a fabric that is glaringly out of sequence. The major disadvantage of a valuefinder is that it does not give the truest reading of red fabrics. In making a general assessment, however, it can be very helpful.
- *Distance* yourself from your fabrics. Colors (and your perception of value) may read differently from a distance. Arrange your fabrics on your worktable, then stand across the room. Do the values read the same?
- *Squint* at your fabric, or consider removing your glasses. The fuzzy results may enable you to focus less on the

fabric's pattern and more on its overall appearance. Each fabric should blur smoothly into its neighbors: if it doesn't, it may be out of place in terms of value.

- *A black and white instant photo* of your fabric arrangement may be helpful if you are still having difficulty.

Making A Fabric Reference Card

When you are satisfied that you have achieved the most accurate arrangement of your fabrics from the lightest to the darkest, take a small clipping of each, in order, and affix it with transparent tape to a sheet of *white* paper or posterboard (plate 4-12, page 61). It helps to slightly overlap the clippings so that you can see how one fabric blends into the next.

Many of my students are amazed when they have completed their fabric reference cards. Fabrics that they thought would *never* fit in seem to blend smoothly into the overall color scheme. The reason for this is twofold:

- By "bridging" or "blending" the colors in your color scheme, you have assured yourself that no single fabric will scream for attention. This is not to say that you may not have some very unusual fabrics, both in color and in visual texture, but you will avoid the visual jarring of a single bright red fabric on a very blue quilt.
- Secondly, it is amazing how different a fabric can look when it is cut into a small piece rather than viewed as a two yard chunk. This is, after all, what a scrap quilt is all about: lots of divergent little pieces, sewn together to create a harmonious whole. By cutting little pieces of each of your fabrics and laying them out before you, you are able to get a much better understanding of how even the most suspicious looking fabrics can work into the big picture.

This *fabric reference card* will be helpful to you in many ways:

- Scrap quilts are frequently built over a long period of time. It may be highly impractical for you to leave all of your chosen fabrics piled in your workspace for the weeks, months (or even years!) that you work on a specific project, especially if your workspace is your guestroom or dining room table. With this fabric card as a reference, you can put the fabrics away if the need arises and a week or month later, using the card, immediately retrieve those fabrics that you had selected for this particular quilt.

- You will have a ready-made reference when shopping for additional fabric or trading fabrics with friends. You will know what you already have and will also be aware of where the shortfalls may be. Are you heavy on the blues but a little light on the greens? Could your zinger use a little support? Would a few geometrics give your selection a little more texture? As you add new fabrics, be sure to clip and integrate them into your fabric reference card.

- When the time comes to sit down and actually begin cutting, arranging and sewing your quilt blocks, the heavy "thinking" will be done. You will know the *relative* value of each fabric in the color scheme you have selected. All you will need to do is cut and go!

Students have often asked, "How do I determine on my reference card where the light fabrics end and the mediums begin?" The answer is that you don't need to! Remember: the value relationships between fabrics are all relative. By arranging your fabrics from lightest to darkest, you know the relative value of every fabric in your color scheme as compared to every other fabric. If you arranged from lightest on the left to darkest on the right, you know that every fabric to the left of a particular fabric is "lighter than," while every fabric to the right is "darker than." It's such an easy way to work! The advantages will become even more apparent as you move into the actual construction phase of your scrap quilt.

CHAPTER 5
Drafting Basics

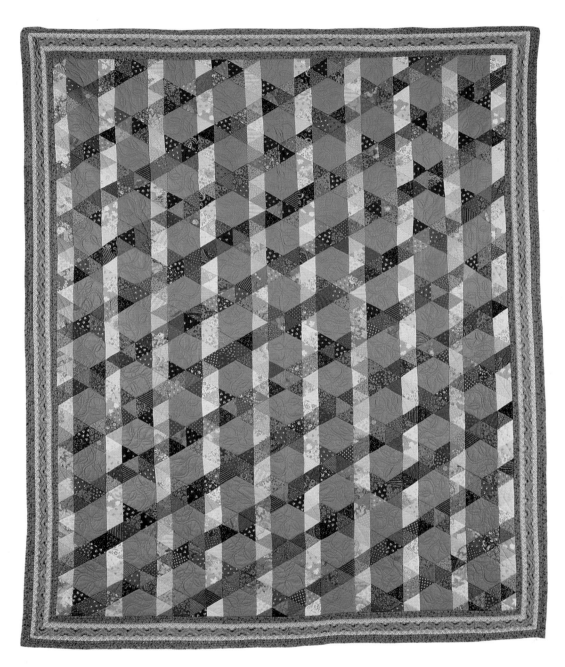

Plate 5-1
LATTICE, 75" x 90", Nan Tournier,
Mt. Pleasant, SC, 1986. The hexagon and
the 60-degree equilateral triangle are the basis
for this wonderful quilt.

DRAFTING BASICS:
DECLARE YOUR QUILTING INDEPENDENCE!

You've chosen a pattern and selected your fabrics with an eye toward color, value and visual texture. Now you are eager to cut and sew. In flipping through the pages of this book, however, you are suddenly aware of a startling omission: there are *no patterns*!

As anyone who has ever been in one of my workshops or classes can readily explain: with extremely rare exception, I never provide patterns for my students, even those in "absolute beginner" classes. To do so, I feel, is to do them a serious injustice, making them unnecessarily dependent on me, other teachers, fellow quilters and/or quilt publications. And yet, students continue to leave my classes with wonderful quilts underway. My phone rings with excited progress reports and my mail frequently includes letters brimming with confidence and pride along with photos of completed projects. How can this be possible if I withhold that all-important piece of the puzzle: the pattern?

The answer is that rather than patterns, I share with my students a skill that I am ever so grateful my very first quilt teacher shared with me: the ability to draft. While some are very reluctant at first – "You *are* kidding? I can't (don't want to, never have tried to) draft!" – almost all are willing to try.

My scrap quilt workshops do not include a formal lesson in drafting. Instead, I work independently with students who need or want patterns they don't have. These impromptu one-on-one drafting sessions invariably draw a crowd. Obviously, the ability to draft is a skill many quiltmakers wish to acquire, but, for whatever reason, are afraid to try. When presented in a simple, step-by-step and encouraging fashion, however, pattern drafting can be enlightening, confidence-inspiring and fun.

That's what this chapter is all about. If you've never drafted before, please read it through and, working along with the instructions and diagrams, give it a try. You'll be surprised at how simple it can be!

Why Draft?

The ability to draft your own patterns is probably one of – if not *the most* – valuable skills you can acquire as a quiltmaker. How many times have you admired a quilt pictured in a book or magazine, only to discover the pattern is for a nine-inch block while you'd prefer a 12-inch version for your queen-sized bed? How often have you searched in vain for the quilt block pattern that you spotted at a museum exhibit or an out-of-town quilt show? If you can draft your own patterns, this need never be a problem.

Drafting most quilt blocks is a very simple process, yet many quiltmakers shy away and spend the entirety of their quilting lives dependent on pre-printed patterns. It's time to declare your quilting independence!

The Key Word: Accuracy

The single most important word to keep in mind when drafting a pattern is the word *accuracy*. A little extra care taken at this point can lead to quilt blocks that fit smoothly together, resulting in a quilt that lies flat and hangs straight. Such a quilt is not only a joy to behold, but also a pleasure to construct.

For best results, be sure your tools are up to the task: sharp pencils, "true" graph paper and an accurate ruler. Take your time and work in good light. Most of all, enjoy the sense of freedom that drafting can bring.

Getting Started: Materials

What follows is a simple explanation of the drafting process. To work along with these instructions, you'll need a few sheets of large ¼-inch (four squares to the inch) graph paper. You can find it in blotter-sized pads at office supply stores or in a convenient 12-inch square size, designed specifically by and for quilters and available at many quilt shops. You'll need a few sharp pencils (a fine lead mechanical pencil works wonderfully), an eraser and an accurate 12- or 18-inch ruler. I keep two on hand for drafting and template making: one metal, with a no-slip cork backing and the other, the see-through gridded variety. To draft simple eight-pointed stars or hexagons you will also need a compass. The thought of a compass may seem scary at first, especially if you have not touched one since high school geometry...but remember, we are going to keep this very simple. Once you have mastered some basic drafting skills, you will have the confidence to tackle more complex designs on your own.

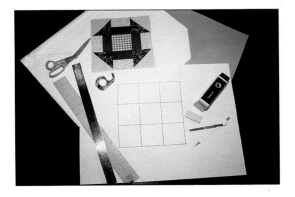

Plate 5-2
Good tools and good light are essential to accurate drafting!

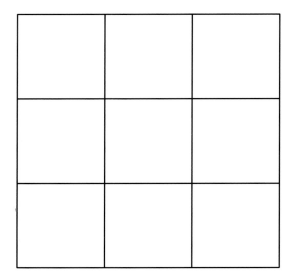

Figure 5-1
A basic nine-patch grid.

We've already established that the most effective pattern for a scrap quilt is often the most simple. Therefore, our focus will be on drafting the four-patch, the nine-patch and the 16-patch, the basic eight-pointed star and the hexagon, which can easily be divided into the 60-degree diamond or triangle. You'll find that the captions accompanying many of the quilts in this book give information to help identify the appropriate drafting "category."

Identifying The Grid: Four-, Nine- Or 16-Patch?

Let's begin by defining the term *grid*. A grid is nothing more than a square divided into smaller, equally sized squares (figure 5-1).

If you look carefully at a variety of popular quilt blocks, including those shown in Chapter 2, you will notice that many of them are based on some type of grid. Let's look more closely at a few of those blocks to determine exactly what type of grid is the basis for each design.

Careful examination of the Pinwheel block (figure 5-2) reveals that if you break the large square down into smaller equal-size square units, you come up with four squares, each composed of two right angle triangles. The Pinwheel, therefore, is a four-patch design based on a four-patch grid.

Following the same process, you can easily see that the Churn Dash (figure 5-3) is based on a nine-patch grid and the Evening Star (figure 5-4) on a 16-patch. Many, many other familiar blocks are based on these three simple grids. Refer back to Chapter 2 (figure 2-1, page 30) and see if you can determine which blocks fit each category.

Of course, many blocks are based on more elaborate grids, such as 25-, 36-, 49- and even 64-patch grids, but for now, we will concentrate on the simple, versatile nine-patch.

Figure 5-2

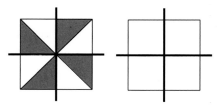

Figure 5-3

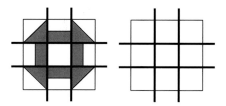

Figure 5-4

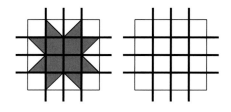

Drawing The Appropriate Grid

The traditional Churn Dash block is a popular choice for scrap quilts. Sarah Porreca has used it as the basis for her quilt DASHING FOR DARRA, pictured in Chapter 2 (plate 2-1, page 27). Let's use this familiar block for our drafting example .

We have already determined that the nine-patch is the grid to use for drafting this particular block. So, to draft it properly, you must begin by drawing a nine-patch grid.

How large should you draw the grid? Unless there is some very specific size I must make my blocks (in order to conform to a very specific overall quilt plan...a rarity for me!), I prefer to draft my block to a size that corresponds mathematically to the appropriate grid. In other words, if I am drafting a 16-patch, such as Evening Star (four squares across by four down), I like to choose a block size that is easily divisible by four, such as eight or 12 inches. This avoids lots of complicated math and messy fractions!

Since the Churn Dash is a nine-patch (three squares across by three down), why not plan the block to a finished size that is easily divisible by three? Nine inches seems a perfect choice.

When the finished size of the block has been determined, the next step is to use an accurate ruler on ¼-inch graph paper to draw a block of the chosen size. Since you have decided on a nine-inch Churn Dash, the block you draw should measure exactly nine inches square.

Now you must divide the large, nine-inch square into the appropriate nine-patch grid of three equal-size squares across by three equal-size squares down. Since you have chosen to do "simple math" (9 ÷ 3 = 3), it is easy to determine that each square in your nine-patch grid will measure three inches (figure 5-5). Use your ruler to draw the vertical and horizontal lines necessary for the appropriate nine-patch grid.

Transferring The Pattern

Once you have the appropriate grid, you can begin to transfer the Churn Dash block to paper so that you can make the templates and begin to cut and sew.

Refer again to the block as pictured in figure 5-3. Begin with the upper left-hand square in your grid, asking yourself, "What must I do on my *grid* to make this square

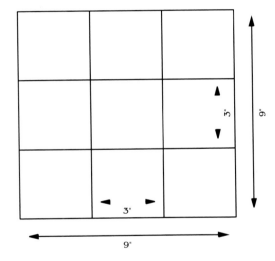

Figure 5-5

Plate 5-3
Transferring the Churn Dash design to the nine-patch grid.

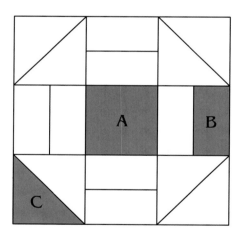

Figure 5-6
The Churn Dash block is composed of three shapes: a square (A), a rectangle (B) and a right angle triangle (C).

correspond with the upper left corner of the block I wish to draw?" In the case of the Churn Dash, you would need to divide the square diagonally into two triangles. Move across to the next square, repeating "What must I do...?" After dividing that square into two equal rectangles, move on, until you have systematically transferred the entire nine squares...and the Churn Dash appears on your grid. That's all there is to it!

If, after drafting the block, you decide that perhaps nine inches is too small and you would prefer a 12-inch block, the situation is easy to correct. Simply begin again, this time drawing the initial square 12 inches instead of nine. Then proceed as described above. The individual squares within the grid will be larger – four inches instead of three – but regardless of the size, the drafting process will remain exactly the same.

Identifying The Number Of Templates

After the pattern has been drawn on graph paper in the desired size, you must determine how many templates (pattern pieces) will be required.

The number of templates you will need depends upon the number of different shapes within your chosen block. Although each Churn Dash block is composed of 17 *pieces*, it contains only three *shapes*: a square (A), a rectangle (B) and a right angle triangle (C), as shown in figure 5-6. I like to shade and letter-label these shapes directly on my graph paper drawing. I find this helps later, when I am ready to actually make my templates.

Determining And Marking Grain Line

Another piece of information I add to my graph paper pattern, and which I will eventually transfer to my finished templates, is the grain line arrow.

A few basic terms should help clear up any confusion about the concept of grain line. The diagram in figure 5-7 will also provide a ready reference.

Grain line refers to the direction of woven threads in a piece of fabric.

Selvage is the tightly woven finished edge of the fabric, often showing the name of the fabric manufacturer or designer.

Lengthwise grain runs parallel to the selvage and has absolutely no stretch at all. *Crosswise grain*, which usually has a bit of give, runs across the fabric, from selvage to selvage. Both lengthwise and crosswise grains are alternately referred to as *straight grain* or *straight of goods*.

Bias is generally considered to be any diagonal line on the fabric. *True bias* is that which runs at a 45-degree angle to the straight of goods. Bias has a great deal of give and a definite tendency to stretch; therefore, it must be handled with care!

When determining how to mark your paper pattern (and eventually your templates) for grain line placement, a good rule of thumb is to keep the straight of goods consistent with the outside edge of the block whenever possible. This will minimize stretching and eliminate the distortion that would occur were bias allowed to fall in this important position. Figure 5-8 indicates reasonable grain line placement for the Churn Dash block.

Note the use of the qualifying words *whenever possible*. There may be times when, for whatever reason, it is not possible to place the straight of goods on the outer edge of a block. For example, you might be working with a specific design motif in a fabric that precludes cutting on the straight of goods. In cases like these, use your best judgment. A "rule of thumb" is not the law!

Adding Seam Allowance: Machine vs. Hand Piecing

If you are planning to machine piece the Churn Dash block, there is one additional step you must take before actually transferring the paper shapes to template material.

Templates designated for machine piecing traditionally have the ¼-inch seam allowance already included. Unlike hand piecing, where the ability to see and follow a sewing guideline is essential, piecing by machine requires an exactly cut, consistent ¼-inch seam allowance. If raw (cut) edges can be matched accurately and effortlessly, you can "train" your sewing machine to measure and sew a perfect ¼-inch seam for you. Therefore templates require an accurate cutting (as opposed to sewing) line for piecing by machine.

To achieve this accurate and consistent ¼-inch seam

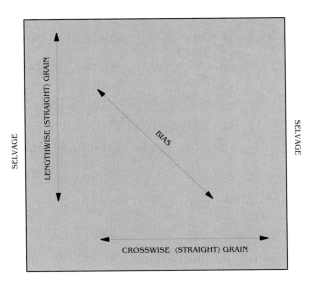

Figure 5-7
Identifying grain line.

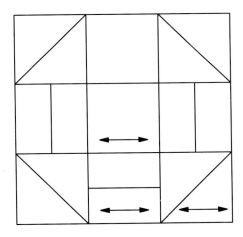

Figure 5-8
Churn Dash block with grain line indicated.

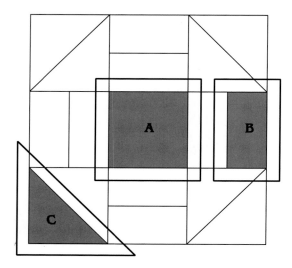

Figure 5-9
Add ¼-inch seam allowance to each shape if you plan to machine piece.

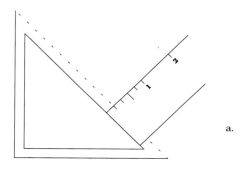

a.

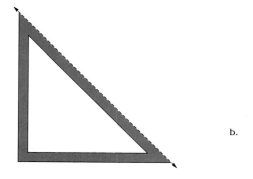

b.

Figure 5-10
Adding diagonal seam allowance to right angle triangle.

allowance in your templates, you will need to add an additional ¼-inch to all sides of each pattern shape (figure 5-9).

Squares and rectangles are rather straightforward. Triangles can be a bit tricky. Use your ruler to add the ¼ inch to the right angle sides of the triangle, extending the "legs" an extra inch or two. Then use your ruler to mark a few key dots ¼-inch out from the diagonal edge of the triangle. Connect the dots and you have the necessary seam allowance on all three sides (figure 5-10). As an alternative, you might use your gridded, see-through ruler to add this diagonal, ¼–inch seam allowance.

If you are planning to piece by hand, you will not need to add seam allowance to your drawing or your templates. Your templates will be made the exact size of each finished piece – the size that already appears in your graph paper drawing – and a ¼-inch seam allowance will be "eyeballed" when you cut your fabric.

Be sure to indicate "hand" or "machine" on each pattern shape in your graph paper rendering. This information will be transferred later, when making the actual templates for the Churn Dash block.

Other Labeling Information

In addition to assigning each individual pattern shape an identifying letter, indicating grain line and specifying for "hand" or "machine" use, I usually add two other pieces of labeling information: the name and the finished size of the overall block.

Putting all of this information on my graph paper drafting serves two purposes:

• It reminds me, at a glance, of my "game plan" should there be a lapse of time between drafting the block and actually making the templates for this particular quilt.

• It jogs my memory as to what key information I want to appear on the actual templates.

**Eight-Pointed Star vs. Nine Patch:
Telling The Difference**

So far, we've talked exclusively about blocks based on a regular grid. While many quilt blocks are based on a regular, equally divisible grid (such as a four-patch or a nine-patch), other commonly used patterns are not. One such popular pattern is the basic eight-pointed star.

At first glance, it may be difficult to tell the difference between a nine-patch star, such as that depicted in Priscilla Hair's VARIABLE STAR (Plate 5-4) and a basic eight-pointed star. But there is a key difference.

Study figure 5-11. In the Variable Star (also called the Ohio Star), the measurements between points A and B, and then B and C are the same. That is because the nine-patch is based on a grid composed of equal size squares.

The Eight-Pointed Star, however, is based on an octagon, an eight-sided shape with all sides equal (figure 5-12). The distance between A and B is equal to the distance between B and D, *not* B and C as in its nine-patch cousin (figure 5-13). Therefore, a different basis must be used to draft the Eight-Pointed Star.

Plate 5-4
VARIABLE STAR, 48" x 48", Priscilla E. Hair, Easley, SC, 1990. The nine-patch version of this traditional block is also known as Ohio Star.

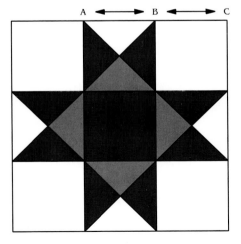

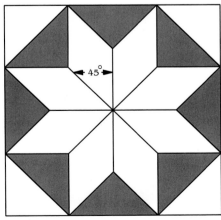

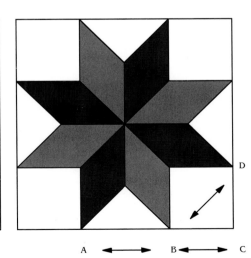

Figure 5-11
The Variable (or Ohio) Star, based on the nine-patch grid.

Figure 5-12
The eight-pointed star is based on an octagon.

Figure 5-13
In an eight-pointed star, the measurement from A to B is equal to the measurement from B to D.

Figure 5-14(a-h)
Drafting the eight-pointed star.

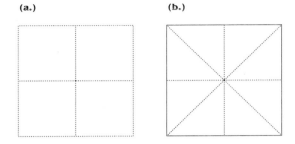

(a.)

(b.)

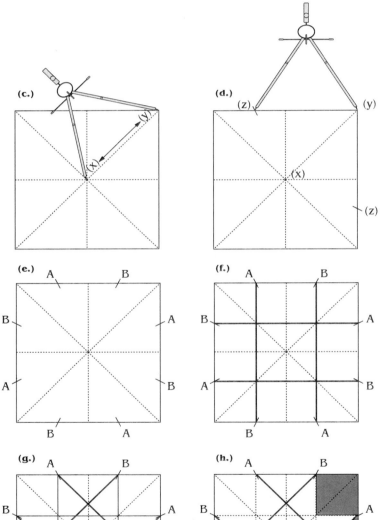

(c.)

(d.)

(e.)

(f.)

(g.)

(h.)

Drafting The Basic Eight-Pointed Star

Because it is not based on an equally divided grid, many quiltmakers are intimidated at the thought of drafting an eight-pointed star. Perhaps it is the unfamiliar compass that shies many from the task. Despite its mystique, drafting the basic eight-pointed star is easy. The numbered illustrations in figure 5-14 will help you as you work.

- As with any block, begin by drawing a square the finished size of the block you desire.

- Using a "light hand," divide the square into four equal quadrants (5-14a), then again on the diagonal in both directions (5-14b). The center point will now be clearly visible.

- Open your compass so that it spans the exact distance from one corner of the block to the center (measurement xy in figure 5-14c). Without changing the measurement, pivot the compass from the corner to the left and the right, making pencil marks where the compass crosses the perimeter of the block (z in figure 5-14d). Repeat from each corner until there are eight marks, two on each side.

- Beginning at the top left and moving clockwise, label the marks A and B on each side (figure 5-14e). Using your ruler, connect all A's with the B's on the *opposite* side of the block (figure 5-14f).

- Finally, connect each A with the "long distance" B on the *adjacent*, or *neighboring* side (figure 5-14g). You will see the diamonds appear. Erase any unnecessary lines to make tracing the three templates (diamond, triangle and square) easier (figure 5-14h).

Once you have become comfortable with using a compass and have mastered drafting the simple eight-pointed star, you may wish to experiment. Blazing Star, Kaleidoscope and Castle Wall are just a few variations on the basic eight-pointed theme. The bibliography at the end of this book contains some excellent resources for exploring further this versatile design.

Drafting The Hexagon

A hexagon is a six-sided, equilateral (all sides equal) shape (figure 5-15). Grandmother's Flower Garden is probably the most commonly recognized of all hexagon based quilt patterns (plate 1-3, page 14).

To draft a hexagon, you must first draw a circle. For purposes of experimentation, let's begin by making the circle – and the resulting hexagon – a random size. Once you are comfortable with the simple mechanics involved, I will explain how you can determine the exact size of the hexagon you wish to draft.

Just follow along with these step-by-step instructions, referring to the numbered drawings in figure 5-16 as you work:

- Open your compass to any random measurement (I find two inches a good size with which to experiment). This measurement will equal the *radius* of your circle (figure 5-16a), and will not be changed throughout the entire drafting process. Carefully hold your compass steady and draw a circle.
- Without changing the measurement, place one point of your compass at any random place on the circle you have drawn. Swing the compass to the left, making a pencil mark that cuts the circle (figure 5-16b).
- Repeat, this time using the mark that you have just made as your starting point (figure 5-16c). Work your way around the entire circumference of the circle until you have made six equidistant marks (figure 5-16d).
- Connect the marks carefully, using your ruler (figure 5-16e). There is your hexagon! Practice a few times until you feel confident handling the compass.

Often, when planning a single-patch scrap quilt, you can simply draft a hexagon to any random size, make a template and begin cutting fabric. There may be occasions, however, when you want your hexagon to finish to a specific size...say, 1½ inches along its side, or five inches at its widest point. How do you draft a hexagon to these specifications?

Figure 5-15
The basic hexagon.

Figure 5-16(a-e)
Drafting the basic hexagon.

(a.)

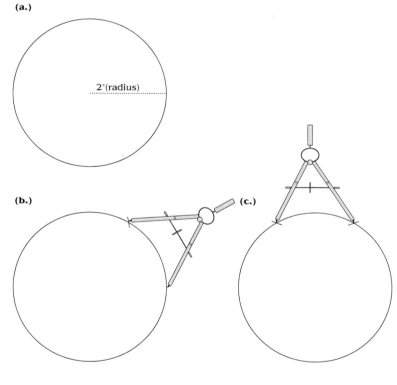

2"(radius)

(b.)

(c.)

(d.)

(e.)

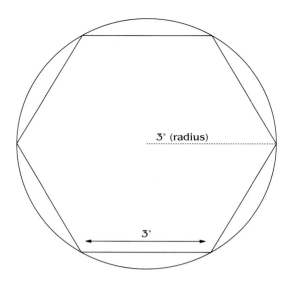

Figure 5-17
Drafting a hexagon to a specific side measurement.

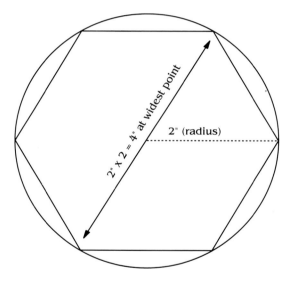

Figure 5-18
Drafting a hexagon to a specific width.

Remember, drafting a hexagon begins with drafting a circle. The answer, therefore, must – and does – lie in the circle! The radius is the key measurement.

• To draft a hexagon to a specific side measurement:

The measurement of the radius of the circle will be equal to the side measurement of the hexagon. If you want a hexagon that will measure three inches on its side, begin the drafting process by opening your compass to draw a circle with a three inch radius (figure 5-17).

• To draft a hexagon to a specific width:

Twice the radius will equal the measurement of the hexagon at its widest point. If you need a hexagon that will measure four inches at its widest point, begin the drafting process by opening your compass to draw a circle with a radius half that figure – in this case, that would be two inches (figure 5-18).

That's all you need to know!

The Hexagon "Subdivided"

In addition to the familiar Grandmother's Flower Garden, there are any number of other quilt patterns based on the hexagon. If you are having trouble thinking of another example, perhaps it is because you have overlooked the variations possible by subdividing the hexagon into different shapes. For example, Priscilla Hair's OCTOBER DAWN, shown in Chapter 2, (plate 2-7, page 32), is based on a pattern called Ecclesiastical or Inner City. The basis for this pattern is a hexagon, divided in half at its widest point (figure 5-19). This is just one of many patterns with its roots in the basic hexagon shape.

As you recall, the hexagon is based on the circle. Thinking back to your days in high school geometry, you may remember that the circle is made up of 360 degrees. The six-sided hexagon breaks that circle down into six equal parts, with six equal angles. By doing some very simple math, you can see that each of those angles equals 60 degrees (360 ÷ 6 = 60). The hexagon, therefore, is the basis for both the 60-degree diamond and the 60-degree triangle, two popular shapes for scrap (and charm) quilt templates.

• The 60-degree diamond

Tumbling Blocks is a favorite pattern based on the 60-degree diamond shape. Look again at the detail of Mary

Underwood's miniature charm quilt TURBULENCE in Chapter 3 (plate 3-3, page 42). Three 60-degree diamonds come together to form a "block," a cube...or a hexagon (figure 5-20)! Any six-pointed star variation likewise includes the 60-degree (hexagon-based) diamond.

To draft the 60-degree diamond shape, begin by drafting a hexagon. Use your ruler to divide the hexagon with a big "X," marking across its widest points as shown in figure 5-21. The 60-degree diamond, basis for Tumbling Blocks, six-pointed stars and other 60-degree diamond variations, will appear as shaded in the illustration.

• The 60-degree triangle

This triangle variation is frequently associated with the Thousand Pyramids design. It is also the basis, when combined with the hexagon, for Nan Tournier's lovely LATTICE (plate 5-1, page 65).

If you have already drafted the 60-degree diamond, you don't need to draft another thing. The leftover shape from your diamond drafting (figure 5-22) *is* a 60-degree triangle!

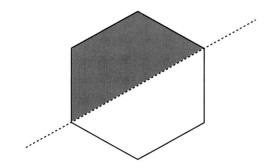

Figure 5-19
The half hexagon.

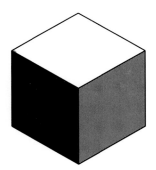

Figure 5-20
Tumbling Block.

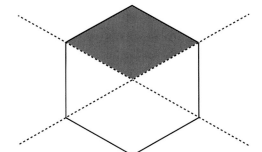

Figure 5-21
The 60-degree diamond.

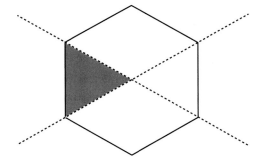

Figure 5-22
The 60-degree
equilateral triangle.

Making Templates

Once you have experimented with drafting the Churn Dash, the basic eight-pointed star and the hexagon shape, you are ready to draft the pattern of your choice and to make the appropriate templates. The tips that follow may be helpful to you.

As scrap quilts usually involve tracing and cutting the same shapes over and over, you will want to use a template material that is durable. The special translucent template plastic available to quilters specifically for this purpose is not only more durable, but also tends to remain more accurate than cardboard or other materials. For this reason, it is my template material of choice. Just be certain that the material is not so slick that it will not retain markings.

To assure the accuracy of your templates, tape your graph paper rendering to your work surface and then tape the template material on top of that. This will prevent either the paper or the plastic from slipping. Little steps like this lead to quilt blocks that fit together. Take the time to do them!

Using a sharp pencil and a ruler, trace one of each pattern shape on to the template material. (Remember: if you are piecing by machine, this pattern piece includes the ¼-inch seam allowance you have marked; if you are piecing by hand, it does not and you are tracing the shape exactly the size it appears in your original block drawing.) Then, using utility scissors, cut each plastic pattern piece *exactly* on the pencil line. You may want to trace and cut one template at a time so that you can move and conserve the template material. Transfer the labeling information from your graph paper drawing to your templates. Be sure to include the name and finished size of the block, the "letter" of the particular shape you are cutting, the position of the grain line and whether seam allowance is included. (Figure 5-23 shows a complete set of properly marked Churn Dash templates.) When you have cut and identified all of the templates for your block, place them in a labeled envelope or plastic food storage bag to keep them handy when not in use.

A Quick Review

In wrapping up this chapter on drafting and templates, let's review a few main points:

- Choose good, accurate drafting materials.
- Work in good light in a comfortable setting.
- Examine your chosen block carefully in terms of a potential grid. Is it a four-patch? A nine-patch? Or is it, perhaps, based on the eight-pointed star?
- Choose a finished size block that makes for "simple math."
- When tracing templates, secure both graph paper and template material with tape to avoid slippage and insure accuracy.
- Label templates with pattern name, finished block size, an identifying letter, grain line arrow and the designation "hand" or "machine."
- Refuse to view the absence of a particular pattern as an obstacle. Consider it a pleasant challenge and have fun – and gain confidence – while drafting your own!

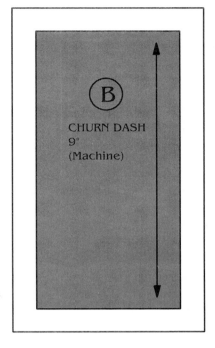

Figure 5-23
Churn Dash templates, labeled for machine piecing.

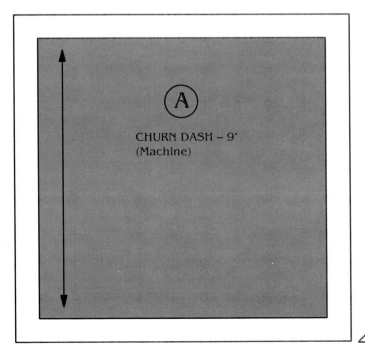

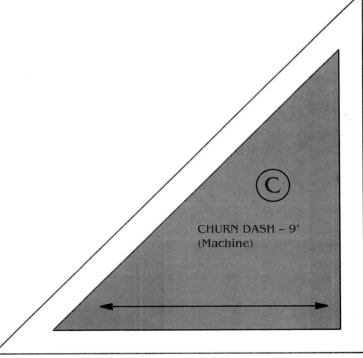

CHAPTER 6
Scrap Quilt Strategies

Plate 6-1
DADDY'S BOW TIES, 55" x 65", Laura Tassin Chapman and Bettydeen "Bunny" Tassin, Charleston, SC 1989-90 (four-patch). Made for a bow tie-wearing gentleman in honor of his 70th birthday. Collection of Max Tassin.

SCRAP QUILT STRATEGIES:
TECHNIQUES FOR CUTTING, DESIGN & CONSTRUCTION

When I am asked to describe my style as a quiltmaker, phrases such as "instinctive," "intuitive" or even "seat-of-the-pants" often come to mind. The thought of pre-planning every detail of a quilt, laboring over the placement of every fabric and doing elaborate scale drawings has never appealed to me. I prefer to do my design work "in the cloth," trying out my ideas directly in fabric. This method involves a willingness to experiment, a certain degree of openmindedness and flexibility, as well as the ability to make a few "spur of the moment" decisions – and rejections! I'll admit, working in this design-as-you-go fashion took a bit of getting used to, but it has led me to some interesting discoveries and added a spontaneity and freedom to my quilts I might not have achieved with lots of advance planning. Now I can't imagine designing a quilt any other way.

Perhaps that is why I feel so comfortable working in the scrap quilt format. Scrap quilts are most successful when they contain an element of spontaneity and surprise. An "overly planned" scrap quilt can quickly become static and uninspired, losing the visual excitement so admired in the quilts of our nineteenth century predecessors.

This is not to say that I do not give some advance thought to the direction my scrap quilt will take. As witnessed in previous chapters of this book, I *do* pre-select a block, explore its design potential with a brief series of black and white sketches and carefully develop a fabric palette with thoughtful eye to color, value and visual texture. Secure in the knowledge that I have done my "homework," however, I am then free to give myself over to the creative process, trusting my preparation, as well as my instinct and a certain amount of serendipity, to lead me to a sensational scrap quilt.

There are many theories regarding scrap quilt design. What follows is the design-as-you-go method that students learn in the scrap quilt workshops I teach. I know it works, not only because I have seen the quilts that result from these workshops – witness many of the quilts in this book! – but also because it is the method that I use in my own workroom.

The Design-As-You-Go Quilt Plan

It is a rare event indeed for me to begin a scrap quilt with the entire quilt planned on paper. My quilts tend to develop naturally after I have sewn six or ten or a dozen blocks. The blocks themselves will often give me direction as to how they might be set, what fabric (or fabrics) to use for setting blocks or sashes, whether or not to include borders and so on.

The only exception is when I am certain in advance that I want to set my blocks side-by-side (with no sashing or plain blocks) to achieve a secondary design discovered while doing my black and white tracing paper overlays. Even so, I do not draw out the whole quilt. Instead, I expand my four-block drawing to perhaps a dozen blocks, mainly to develop a sense of the size. I do not plan border treatments at this stage. In fact, even my side-by-side set is subject to change once I begin to make the blocks, should they dictate otherwise. That is one of the great enjoyments of making a scrap quilt: wonderful things can happen as the quilt begins to take shape. Remember to remain open-minded to alternatives.

You may be feeling rather uncertain at the thought of cutting and piecing blocks with no precise plan as to how these blocks will finish to fit a full-sized bed – or to any pre-determined size. There is no need to worry: after completing a dozen blocks, you can usually assess the situation, determine a set and border, and by making the necessary balance of blocks, get a quilt to within a reasonable target size. If this is a little *too* free-form a design method for you, you might want to try a rough sketch. Avoid, however, the comfort of pre-planning every specific detail on paper. If you set up too many rules now, you may feel guilty about breaking them later, even if for the betterment of your quilt.

The Design Wall

In order to experiment with the "design as you go" method, you will need to set aside space in your workplace for a design wall. This can be as simple or elaborate, limited or spacious, temporary or permanent as your personal circumstances allow. Suggestions for creating a design wall in your workspace follow later in this section.

A design wall enables you to cut and "play" with various fabric arrangements within a quilt block before the block is actually sewn together. Because of its surface, fabric shapes can be cut and rearranged with no pinning necessary. Finished blocks can be tested in various arrangements before the entire quilt top is sewn or "set."

With a design wall you are better able to maintain a proper visual perspective on your work. Laying quilt blocks on the floor or bed often distorts the appearance of the blocks furthest away. A design wall eliminates this problem.

Finally, while providing a blank, unintrusive background, a design wall enables you to distance yourself from your work, allowing you to determine whether your fabrics are performing as intended in terms of color, value and visual texture.

These are just some of the advantages of working on a design wall. You will probably find many more as you proceed with the cutting and construction of your quilt top. In fact, once you have used the design wall to "try out" your design ideas, you will probably never make another quilt without it!

How can you have a design wall in your workspace?

- It can be as simple as a 36-inch square of cotton batting, white felt or flannel pinned or taped to the wall. My design wall is a 72-inch square of white felt, attached to the wall with push pins. I found the felt, 72 inches wide on the bolt, tucked in a distant corner of my local fabric shop. It was an easy, inexpensive but extremely effective solution to my designing dilemma.

- For a more portable arrangement, try stapling a large piece of felt or flannel over stretcher bars like an artist's canvas. You can even carry this design "wall" to workshops and classes.

- Some quiltmakers, especially those with sewing rooms or studios that are completely their own, prefer a more permanent arrangement. Celotex®, available in large sheets at a lumber yard or building supply store, can be covered with felt or flannel and fixed more permanently to the wall. An added advantage to the Celotex® is that it can serve double duty as a bulletin board. Sketches, fabric swatches and photographs can be attached to the design surface with thumb tacks, pins or push pins.

Designing "In The Cloth": The Individual Blocks

Once you have done all the "thinking" work (selected a block, done a few black and white overlays, chosen your

Plate 6-2
Black and white sketch, fabrics, templates, fabric reference card...all the "thinking" work is done. Now you are ready to play!

fabric and made your templates) you are ready to begin cutting the fabric and designing and sewing your quilt top. In essence, it's time to play!

Using the Churn Dash block as an example once again, let's walk through the design-as-you-go process just as I use it when designing scrap quilts in my workroom. Once you have a basic feel for the process, you can put it to work on the block of your choice. You'll be amazed at how easy and exciting it can be!

I begin designing my scrap quilt by going back to the original black and white sketches of the block with which I have chosen to work. Selecting one configuration, I plan to make enough blocks in that particular configuration to establish the pattern in my quilt. For our example, I will focus on the Churn Dash configuration showing the background as light, the churn dash itself as dark and the center square as medium in value (figure 6-1).

Next, I go to my fabrics and begin cutting. I cut a stack of rectangles and triangles from a variety of my lighter fabrics to use for the backgrounds, a stack of rectangles and triangles from my darks for the actual churn dashes and a stack of medium squares for the centers.

I pay no attention to *color* at this time...I just choose fabrics from the lighter, medium and darker ranges of my fabric palette, using my fabric reference card as a guide.

When I have cut enough fabric for a number of blocks (usually about six or eight), I begin to "play" on my design wall. Generally, I work on four blocks at a time. First, I place four medium centers. Then I go to my darks and choose a churn dash to place around each center. Finally, I place a light background in each block. Having cut more pieces than I need at the moment, I have a bit of flexibility in fine tuning the four blocks on my design wall. The leftover pieces can be set aside for use in later blocks. Plate 6-3 shows my design wall with my original black and white sketch and four Churn Dash blocks, cut and arranged in my favored configuration.

Note that I have chosen my fabrics rather randomly, based only on their value. I do not cut each block individually or plan as I cut..."Now, this light will be the background for that dark churn dash...it matches so well!" I just place light, medium and dark pieces in their

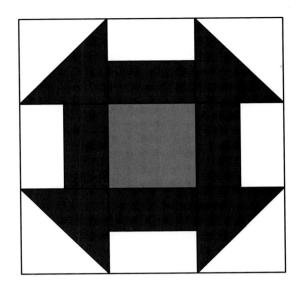

Figure 6-1
The chosen configuration.

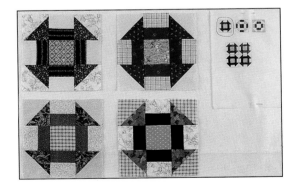

Plate 6-3
My design wall with four Churn Dash blocks in the chosen configuration.

assigned places on the design wall, using my black and white sketch as a guide. After giving considerable thought to selecting my fabrics, with careful attention to color and texture, I can feel assured that, at this point, even a somewhat random approach will yield satisfactory results.

The "Maverick" Block: Scrambling The Formula

Once I have arranged four blocks in my chosen configuration, and have firmly established the pattern of the quilt, I begin to "play around" with the block design. In one out of each four blocks, I will scramble the formula of my black and white sketch. Perhaps, I will cut and substitute a fabric of more medium value for the background in one of the blocks, or I will replace the medium center with a darker fabric. Plate 6-4 shows my design wall with the same four Churn Dash blocks, only this time one has had the values scrambled.

Changing the *value* placement (while not necessarily the *color*) of even a single fabric can totally alter the appearance of a block. Sometimes, the original pattern may disappear and a new design element emerge. The resulting block may not be as "pretty" as some of the other, more conforming blocks, but it will add the visual excitement I know my scrap quilt needs to be successful.

If you are wary of the effect these "maverick" blocks will have on the finished quilt, you need only to study the photographs of the scrap quilts in this book. The occasional shift of values within the chosen block is not nearly as disruptive as you might expect. In fact, it actually adds to the impact of the quilt. A few "maverick" blocks will keep the viewer's eye moving over the quilt's surface. Ruth Templeton's STAR LIGHT, STAR BRIGHT (plate 6-5) and Sarah Porreca's DASHING FOR DARRA (Plate 6-6), both pictured in Chapter 2 and detailed here, are excellent examples. Each of these quilts is a feast for the eye; there is always something new to discover and explore.

Sometimes these "maverick" blocks are unique in that they maintain a very low profile in the overall quilt. They may contain very little contrast in the value of the fabrics within the block – so much so that the pattern almost disappears, as it does in occasional blocks in DADDY'S BOW TIES (plate 6-1, page 81). Or, they may blend into the background of setting blocks or sashes by

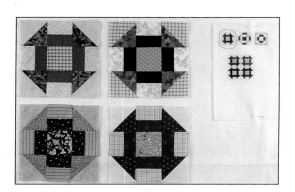

Plate 6-4
Four Churn Dash blocks...including one "maverick"!

Plate 6-5
STAR LIGHT, STAR BRIGHT, Ruth Templeton,
detail.

Plate 6-6
DASHING FOR DARRA, Sarah Porreca, detail.
The occasional shifting of values within the
block makes for a more visually exciting quilt.

Plate 6-7
FRATERNAL TWIN I, 51" x 55½",
by the author, 1989-90. Based on the
traditional Shoofly block (nine-patch).
A multiple prizewinner. Collection of
Matthew Brown.

virtue of the fabrics in them. FRATERNAL TWIN I (plate 6-7) contains examples of both low contrast and "blend into the background" blocks.

"Low profile" blocks are quite common in older scrap quilts. The early twentieth century GRANDMOTHER'S FLOWER GARDEN shown in Chapter 1, is a case in point. Many modern quiltmakers, however, tend to shy away from them, fearful of altering a quilt's formula once it is set. No need to worry! As long as there are enough blocks in a uniform configuration to establish the pattern, the viewer will read that pattern in the quilt and automatically "fill in the blanks" even when the design is not obviously visible. The result, meantime, is a much more interesting quilt surface.

How many "mavericks" and/or "low profiles" per quilt? That's up to you! Sometimes, besides my one-in-four, I'll add an extra one or two late in the design stage – just for good measure! On average, therefore, between one-quarter and one-third of my blocks stray from the original formula. The final decision depends upon many factors: the complexity of the pattern, the ultimate size of the quilt, my sense of adventure on a particular day. I'll admit I started out a bit shy when it came to these oddball blocks, but quickly overcame reticence when I saw the results.

Please keep in mind when dealing with "maverick" blocks that not every individual block in a quilt need be pretty. Some blocks you will undoubtedly like more than others. Remember the "big picture" concept. One or two ugly ducklings, while seemingly unattractive when viewed in isolation, can provide just the touch of personality needed to liven up an entire quilt top! (See plate 6-8.)

I think it is important to note that there is an occasional exception to my "scramble the formula, maverick block" approach. The exception usually occurs when I have preplanned a side-by-side set and I am counting on a specific secondary design to be established by consistent placement of values within each block. In that case, I will scramble with a somewhat more restrained hand. Learn to trust your judgment!

Starting To Sew

Once I have arranged four blocks (including my "maverick") on the design wall and am satisfied with my

Plate 6-8
APPALACHIAN SPRING, detail. Trish Gabriel has included some unusual fabrics in her quilt. Not every block might be called "pretty," but the overall effect, shown in full in Chapter 9, is a visually striking quilt!

choices, I proceed to my sewing machine (or needle and thread if I am planning to piece by hand).

This is an important step. Because of the endless fabric combinations possible in a scrap quilt, it is all too easy to become obsessed with "what if?" and to try every conceivable option before beginning to sew. *Resist this temptation* or you (and your quilt) will remain frozen on the design wall. As soon as you have arrived at four blocks that catch your fancy, start sewing. Construct the four blocks (but do not join them together yet). One of the greatest pleasures of the scrap quilt, both in the viewing and the making, is that every block is a surprise. With the design-as-you-go method, you are never far from the next delicious discovery.

The Special Role Of Medium Value Fabrics

Sometimes quiltmakers are not certain how to use medium value fabrics in their quilt blocks, especially when the pattern (for example, Log Cabin or Thousand Pyramids) seems to call for strong contrast between light and dark. As a result, they tend to stay safely with the lightest lights and the darkest darks and then are disappointed when the resulting quilt "falls flat."

The skillful use of medium value fabric is another tool to help you in developing a sensational scrap quilt. Remember: the operative word when considering the value of fabric is *relative*. Each medium value fabric in your selected color scheme is light compared to the darker fabrics, but dark compared to the lighter ones. These versatile mediums can fill a variety of roles in your quilt, and having carefully arranged your fabrics in relative value order on your fabric reference card, you are in a perfect position to take advantage of this versatility.

Experiment! Try occasionally replacing a light fabric in your block with one or more medium values. Just be sure that the medium you choose is lighter than the darks already in place so that the visual contrast remains intact. In another block, try substituting one of your darker mediums for true dark. Sometimes, for fun, I will use the same medium fabric in two different blocks – one time working as a light, then replacing a dark, as in CEDAR LAKES AUTUMN (plate 6-9, page 91).

Again, don't be shy about making these

Plate 6-9
CEDAR LAKES AUTUMN, 43" x 45", by the author, 1990-91. (Flying Geese, traditional.) Using the same fabric sometimes as a "light," sometimes as a "dark," adds to the visual interest of the quilt. Note, for example, the pink fabrics in this quilt and how they are placed alternately in the light, then dark position.

substitutions! Since you are using your design wall to experiment, you can always change your mind before you make the commitment to sew. I think, however, that you will be amazed at the movement and element of surprise these variations can add to your quilt.

A Certain Look: The Use Of Muslin

Some quiltmakers like the calming effect that muslin, used as a background, sashing or setting fabric, can have on a busy scrap quilt. For many, it provides a comfortable way to ease the transition from quilts composed of four or five coordinated fabrics to the scrap quilt format with its hundreds of diverse prints. Others admire the look of the scrap quilts of the 1920's, 1930's and 1940's and rely on muslin to capture that look.

Although I never use it in my own scrap quilts, preferring instead the challenges and resulting richness of texture inherent in print fabric, I have seen some beautiful examples, old and new, which use muslin as an important design element. You'll find a number of these wonderful quilts throughout this book to provide you with inspiration.

Simplifying The Task: Cutting And Construction Tips

It is not my plan to give specific basic instruction for hand or machine piecing here. Many fine books already in print cover the subject very thoroughly and effectively. You will find some of these books listed in the bibliography at the end of Chapter 10.

I do, however, plan to include a few tips and hints to make the cutting and overall construction of your scrap quilt more efficient and satisfying.

Keep in mind that whatever method you choose – with or without templates, scissors or rotary cutter, hand or machine pieced – it is important to exercise care when marking, cutting and sewing. Attention to technique results in scrap quilts that are sensational in workmanship as well as design.

• HOORAY FOR THE ROTARY CUTTER:

(Note: These rotary cutting techniques work only if you are planning to machine piece since rotary cut pieces *include* seam allowance. If you are planning to hand piece, you will still need to hand trace every piece. You can,

Plate 6-10
WHEEL OF FORTUNE, 86" x 104½",
Marietta Breidenthal, Banner Elk, NC, 1988-89.
The quiltmaker has used unbleached muslin
as a consistent, restful background for her
traditional Wheel of Fortune (four-patch)
blocks.

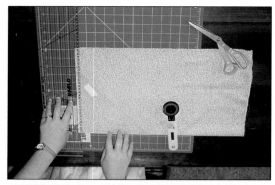

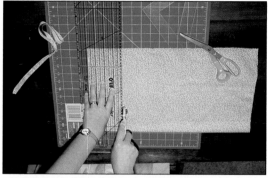

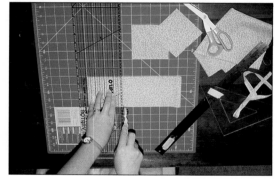

Plate 6-11(a-c)
Using the rotary cutter to cut squares.

however, save cutting time by using your rotary cutter and gridded ruler in place of scissors, adding a ¼ inch seam allowance as you cut.)

Although my design-as-you-go method of scrap quilt construction does not allow for many of the speed piecing techniques some quilters favor, don't despair. You needn't consign your rotary cutter to mothballs! Here's how to put it to vigorous use – and to save time as well.

Regardless of how you plan to cut your quilt blocks, draft your chosen pattern as described in Chapter 5. Once the design is on paper, study it. See which pieces, if any, are suitable for cutting without templates by use of the rotary cutter.

Any units that are square can easily be rotary cut. Refer to your graph paper rendering to determine the *finished* size of the square you need. Then simply add a half-inch to both length and width and cut your square to that size. For example, if your nine-inch Churn Dash block calls for a three-inch center square, use your rotary cutter to cut a 3½ inch square (figure 6-2). If you need more than one square the same size from the same fabric, you can cut a strip the *finished* width plus ½ inch and then cut the strip down into squares, as illustrated in plate 6-11(a-c).

The rotary cutter can also be used to cut rectangles. For the same nine-inch Churn Dash block, you will need rectangles to finish 1½ x 3 inches. Just add ½ inch to each measurement (2 x 3½ inches) and cut (figure 6-3, below). The strip cutting method described for squares can also be applied here.

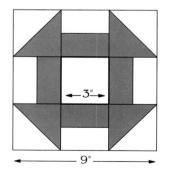

3" + ½" = 3 ½"

3 ½"

3 ½"

3"

9"

Figure 6-2

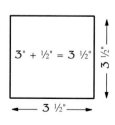

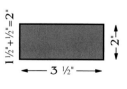

3"

1 ½"

1½" + ½" = 2"

2"

3 ½"

9"

Figure 6-3

Even triangles can be cut without templates using the rotary cutter. For half-square triangles such as those found in the corners of the Churn Dash block, use the following formula: After determining the *finished* size of the pieced square, add ⅞ inch (figure 6-4, below). Cut a square to that measurement and divide on the diagonal (plate 6-12, right). Presto: two half-square triangles!

Some blocks, such as the Ohio or (nine-patch) Variable Star, include a unit composed of four triangles sewn along right angle edges to form a square. To rotary cut these triangles, you must determine the *finished* size of the square and add 1¼ inches (figure 6-5). Cut a square to that measurement and then divide diagonally in both directions. You'll be cutting a big X as shown in plate 6-13.

The more you use your rotary cutter, the more ways you will find to use it. It has many applications beyond the obvious Log Cabin and Irish Chain. Even though you can't do much speed piecing with the design-as-you-go method, think of the time you can save by not tracing around and cutting individual squares and triangles with a template!

• CHAIN PIECING: CONSERVE TIME AND THREAD

When piecing by machine, you can save time and thread by employing a stitching method called *chain piecing*. To chain piece, pin and stack like units, such as the right triangles that must be joined to form the corner squares of the Churn Dash block. Begin sewing, but do not backstitch or clip the thread between units. Instead, continue to feed the units in a continuous chain, pausing

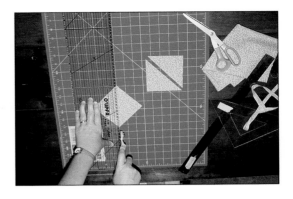

Plate 6-12
Using the rotary cutter to cut half-square triangles.

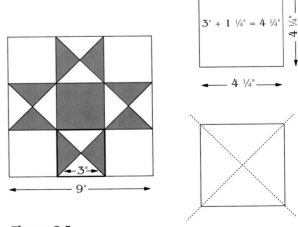

Plate 6-13
Using the rotary cutter to cut quarter-square triangles.

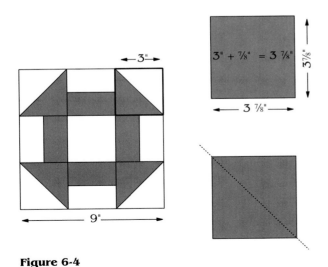

Figure 6-4

3" + ⅞" = 3 ⅞"

3 ⅞"

3 ⅞"

Figure 6-5

3" + 1 ¼" = 4 ¼"

4 ¼"

4 ¼"

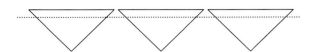

Figure 6-6
Chain piecing.

to separate them only when they have all been sewn (figure 6-6).

• ONE-PATCH STRATEGY: UNIT CONSTRUCTION

When working with a one-patch unit such as a hexagon or a diamond, it helps to find a larger unit into which a number of one-patch pieces can be sewn. This requires expanding the perception of the "block" beyond the square. For example, in a one-patch quilt, the "block" may be triangular. Think of the equilateral triangle that makes up the Thousand Pyramids design. You might consider stacking six of these triangle patches into one larger equilateral triangle "block," alternating a light and dark triangle as the "peak" (figure 6-7).

Mary Underwood used the unit construction method when assembling her wallhanging TURBULENCE, pictured in Chapter 2. Figure 6-8 shows the unit she used in constructing the center portion of this delightful quilt.

There are two major advantages to the "block" method of assembly for the one-patch quilt as opposed to sewing patch to patch, forming and then joining rows:

• It is much easier to work on the design wall arranging and rearranging "blocks" than it is to work with many individual one-patch pieces.

• As your quilt develops, you can continue to add new fabrics and still maintain the balance of your quilt top.

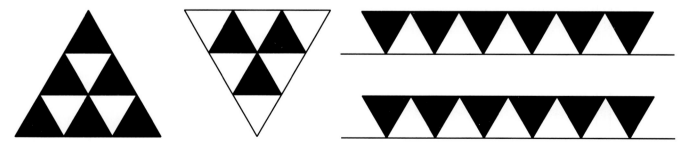

Figure 6-7
Thousand Pyramids: piecing strategy.
"Block units" make for easier assembly than rows.

Should you decide your quilt would benefit from the addition of another color, or you just find more fabrics that reinforce your current color scheme, you can include them in new "blocks" and simply reshuffle the block arrangement. All of the new additions are not clumped conspicuously in one place as they might be if you began sewing rows of individual triangles or diamonds.

Putting It Together...

If you have truly committed yourself to the design-as-you-go method of constructing blocks on a design wall with no overall quilt plan in mind, you will probably find yourself totally immersed in – and delighted with – the process. Eventually, however, after completing ten, or a dozen or fifteen blocks, curiosity takes hold. What will the blocks look like when joined together? How might they be arranged? What are the color and design possibilities for sashing and sets? It's time to examine those possibilities...you are ready for the next step!

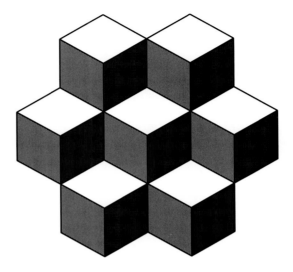

Figure 6-8
TURBULENCE: piecing strategy.

CHAPTER 7
Choosing A Set

Plate 7-1
WINTER STAR, 50" x 50", by the author, 1989.
A combination of two traditional (16-patch)
blocks. Collection of Carley Anne Morreale.

CHOOSING A SET: REVIEWING THE OPTIONS

As mentioned earlier, I frequently begin a scrap quilt with no idea as to the eventual set. Usually, by the time I have completed eight or ten or a dozen blocks, an idea has developed as to how these particular blocks might best be showcased.

Scrap quilts can be set in an endless variety of ways, many reminiscent of the nineteenth century tradition. A number of those possibilities will be covered here, but I strongly encourage you to use your design wall for "play" once you have completed a number of blocks. Sometimes just by arranging and rearranging, turning your blocks this way and that, you will discover a set possibility that would never have occurred to you otherwise. Plate 7-2 shows my design wall with a Bow Tie quilt currently in progress. In addition to the piece partially assembled, you can see some of the various other sets I tried before arriving at my ultimate decision.

Whichever set you choose, be sure that you have pieced all of your blocks before you begin to join or "set" them together. This allows you to achieve overall visual balance in your quilt by controlling placement of color, as well as "maverick" and "low profile" blocks.

Straight Sets

BLOCK-TO-

BLOCK

Figure 7-1

This set is achieved when blocks are set side-by-side, with no sashing or plain blocks in between. One of the biggest advantages to this particular set is the myriad of secondary and even tertiary designs that sometimes develop where the blocks meet. (Refer back to Chapter 3 for a "refresher" on how the block-to-block set can add excitement to your quilt.)

Extreme accuracy is essential when piecing a block-to-block set as there are no sashes or plain blocks to "forgive" seams that don't quite meet. Take the time to

Plate 7-2
Bow Tie quilt with alternate set possibilities, shown in progress on the author's design wall.

piece carefully; the visual excitement of this set is worth the extra effort! Nan Tournier's EDISTO WAVES (plate 7-3) is a perfect example.

BLOCKS

SEPARATED BY

SASHING

Figure 7-2

Plate 7-3
EDISTO WAVES, 44" x 54", Nan Tournier, Mt. Pleasant, SC, 1987. Included in the invitational exhibit "New Quilts for an Old Millennium" at Arrowmont, Gatlinburg, TN, 1987.

This set employs sashing (alternately called *lattice* or *stripping*) to separate the pieced blocks. The sashing may be either plain or pieced, with or without corner squares at its junctions. STAR LIGHT, STAR BRIGHT by Ruth Templeton (see Chapter 2, plate 2-4) effectively demonstrates this particular setting arrangement.

An interesting effect can be achieved when the fabric chosen for sashing matches the background fabric in the individual blocks. The design seems to "float" on the surface of the quilt. You will find an exquisite example of this setting technique in Darlene Christopherson's EVENING STAR, pictured in the next chapter, (plate 8-4).

A good rule of thumb for determining width for sashing is "no wider than one fourth the width of the finished block" (e.g., a three-inch sash for a 12-inch block). Of course, this is just a guideline which can be altered if a specific quilt calls for a different treatment.

PIECED BLOCKS

ALTERNATED WITH

PLAIN BLOCKS

Figure 7-3

Plate 7-4
VARIABLE STARS, 42" x 53 ½", Debbie Steinberg, Blowing Rock, NC, 1991. Based on the 16-patch version of the traditional block.

Debbie Steinberg's VARIABLE STARS (plate 7-4) is a fine example of the "pieced block alternated with the plain block" set, as is the nineteenth century COUNTRY CROSSROADS shown in Chapter 1, (plate 1-2). When

Figure 7-5
Evening (or Variable) Star and Snowball.

Figure 7-6
The two alternating blocks in HIDDEN STARS are actually a "positive-negative" coloration of the Square within a Square block (four-patch).

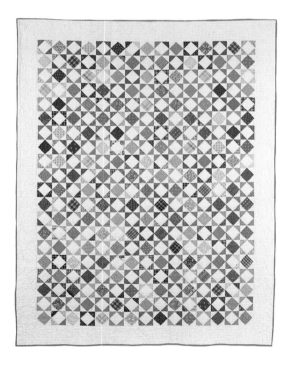

Plate 7-5
HIDDEN STARS, 74" x 92", Sarah Porreca, Hillsborough, NC, 1989. Collection of Karol Schoenbaum.

working with a block containing many fabrics and/or many small pieces, this set can save the quilt from confusion, giving the eye a peaceful place to rest. It also allows the skillful quilter a place to demonstrate her talent and, like the sashed setting, can be a bit forgiving of the less-than-perfect piecer.

All of the plain blocks need not be cut from the same fabric. Variety, in fact, can add to the visual interest of the quilt. This freedom is part of the charm of scrap quilts: if you run out of one fabric, you can simply substitute another!

TWO PIECED

BLOCKS

ALTERNATED

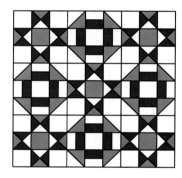

Figure 7-4

Many simple blocks can be used in this set with dramatic results. The tracing paper overlay method, described in Chapter 3, is a good way to experiment.

When alternating two different blocks, it helps if both are based on the same grid (e.g., nine-patch with nine-patch, 16-patch with 16-patch, etc.) so that seams come together in a visually pleasing manner. I like to choose one block with an obviously diagonal line. WINTER STAR (plate 7-1, page 99), a combination of the traditional Evening Star and Snowball blocks (figure 7-5), is a good example.

An interesting variation on the two block design is shown in figure 7-6. HIDDEN STARS by Sarah Porreca demonstrates how a "positive-negative" interpretation of the same block can yield appealing results (plate 7-5).

Diagonal Sets

A diagonal set is what results when a square block is turned "on its ear" or "on point" (figure 7-7, page 103). Turning a square on the diagonal can give even the humblest of quilt blocks a totally new look.

Constructing the diagonal set is easy! Rows are

pieced diagonally, rather than horizontally or vertically and are finished off with squares, half-triangles and quarter-triangles that are based on the finished size of the pieced block (figure 7-8).

The key measurement in a diagonally set block is from "point to point" (figure 7-9). To determine this measurement, multiply the finished side of the block by 1.414. A 12-inch block, therefore, would measure 16.97 inches across its diagonal (12 inches x 1.414 = 16.968), rounded to 17 inches.

You'll need this diagonal measurement later to figure the finished size of your quilt.

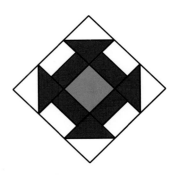

Figure 7-7
The Churn Dash turned "on point."

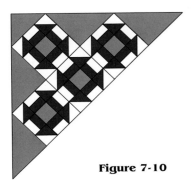

Figure 7-10

BLOCK-TO-

BLOCK

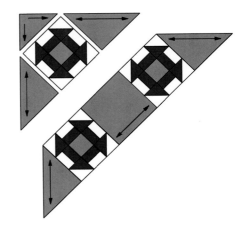

Figure 7-8
Assembling the diagonal set.

This set is achieved when a square block is turned "on point" and set block-to-block, with no plain squares or sashing to separate the blocks. Plain half- and quarter-triangles may be used around the edges to square the top before borders are added.

Like the block-to-block straight set, this set requires extreme precision in piecing.

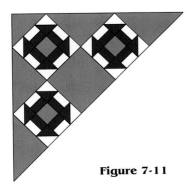

Figure 7-11

PIECED BLOCK

ALTERNATED

WITH PLAIN

BLOCK

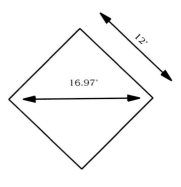

16.97"

12"

12" x 1.414 = 16.97 (17")

Figure 7-9

This set differs from the block-to-block diagonal set in that plain blocks are alternated with the pieced blocks for a more restful appearance. This set requires fewer

Plate 7-6
VARIABLE STAR, 48" x 48", Priscilla E. Hair, Easley, SC, 1990. The nine-patch version of this traditional block is also known as Ohio Star.

a.

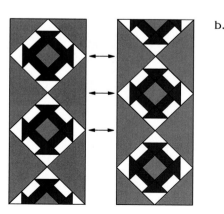
b.

Figure 7-13(a-b)
Assembling the Streak of Lightning set.

pieced blocks and allows plenty of space for quilting in the open areas.

Sarah Porreca's DASHING FOR DARRA, shown in Chapter 2, as well as VARIABLE STAR by Priscilla Hair (plate 7-6), are both fine examples of this set.

STREAK OF

LIGHTNING

SET

Figure 7-12

This is one of my personal favorites. In this set, pieced blocks are turned "on point" and joined in vertical rows. Each row is finished with the necessary half- and quarter-triangles. Rows are staggered before joining to form the lightning or zigzag effect (figure 7-13).

Some quiltmakers avoid this set because they are intimidated by the pieced half-blocks which start and finish every other row. Not to worry: simply draft the full block, divide it on the diagonal, determine what new shapes are formed, add the necessary seam allowances and proceed to piece the half blocks. (*Note*: You cannot take a full pieced block and divide it in half from corner to corner to make a half block...you'll lose the diagonal seam allowance. You must make templates and construct a true half-block.)

Try this one! The extra effort is amply rewarded as evidenced by Martie Culp's wonderful FLYING GEESE AT CEDAR LAKES (plate 7-7).

The "Strippie" Or Bar Set

A "strippie" or bar quilt is a quilt composed of a series of vertical fabric rows, joined together to make a quilt top. In its simplest form, each row is composed of a single strip of fabric, while in more elaborate versions, the rows may be comprised of a series of pieced blocks.

Plate 7-7
FLYING GEESE AT CEDAR LAKES, 42" x 42",
Martie Culp, Wheeling, WV, 1990-91.
This wallhanging, a perfect example of the
Streak of Lightning set, is based on the
traditional Dutchman's Puzzle block
(16-patch)...a "first cousin" to Flying Geese.

In either case, the look of the "strippie" or bar quilt is distinctly vertical and provides a wide variety of alternative set possibilities for the scrap quilt.

VERTICAL ROWS

OF REPEAT

STRAIGHT SET

BLOCKS

Figure 7-14

When separated by plain or striped sashing, this is probably the most familiar of the "strippie" sets. The simple Flying Geese pattern (plate 7-8) is the ideal example.

Plate 7-8
BERYL'S CHALLENGE, 24" x 25", Mary Underwood, Blowing Rock, NC, 1991. (Flying Geese, traditional.) Collection of Beryl Eldring.

VERTICAL ROWS

OF REPEAT

DIAGONALLY SET

BLOCKS

Figure 7-15

This set is the same as the one described above, only this time the blocks are set "on point" within each row. The addition of plain or striped sashing reinforces the vertical line of this attractive set.

FRATERNAL TWIN I, shown in full in the previous chapter, is a good illustration of how effective this set can be. The traditional Shoofly block has been turned on the diagonal and set in rows separated by a complementary striped fabric. Plate 7-9, page 107 details the set.

Figure 7-16

THE
COMBINATION
"STRIPPIE"
SET

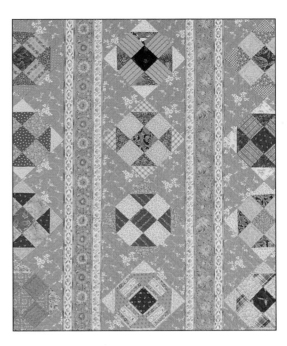

Plate 7-9
FRATERNAL TWIN I, detail. See page 88, plate 6-7, for a full view of this quilt.

Imagine a quilt set in a series of vertical rows, each one showcasing a different block. In one row the block may be straight set; in the next row turned on the diagonal. Any combination will do, so long as the overall set remains vertical, with perhaps a plain or striped sashing to separate the rows.

Experiment! Let your creativity soar. This "strippie" variation offers the ultimate in setting possibilities. You can experiment with three or four different blocks, both straight and diagonal sets, all in the same quilt!

Play Before You Sew!

This chapter contains a wide variety of possible sets for your scrap quilt, but by no means covers all of the alternatives. Perhaps you have a favorite that is not even listed. That doesn't mean it won't work...you just need to "try it out" on your design wall.

Your design wall can play a major role in helping to determine the set for your quilt. Allow yourself the freedom to play. Sometimes the most unlikely experiment reveals the perfect set!

CHAPTER 8
The Use Of Borders

Plate 8-1
NIGHT SKY, 80" x 86", Nan Tournier,
Mt. Pleasant, SC, 1984-90.
This dramatic medallion-style multifabric quilt
was suggested by the traditional Star of
Bethlehem (eight-pointed star). A blue ribbon
winner at the Asheville (NC) Quilt Show, 1991.

THE USE OF BORDERS:
FRAMING YOUR QUILT

A border can serve many purposes for a quilt. This statement holds as true today as it did 100 years ago. Whether it is intended to frame or contain the central design area, created to carry an important design element to the quilt's outer edge, or added simply to enlarge the quilt to fit a specific bed, a carefully chosen, well-proportioned border can enhance and strengthen a quilt's overall impact.

When it comes to choosing a border treatment for your scrap quilt, options abound. Select the option that feels comfortable to you. Learn to trust your eye and your instincts. There are no rules.

The Option Of No Borders

Many nineteenth century quiltmakers settled the question of borders by opting for no borders at all (figure 8-1). The blocks simply spill over to the edge of the quilt and are finished with binding.

While this option is certainly acceptable – and indeed well substantiated by the scrap quilts of the nineteenth century – I generally employ some type of border treatment for my scrap quilts, preferring the frame that a border provides. If, however, you like the "old-timey" look of a borderless quilt, try it. The no border option may be just the solution for your particular quilt.

Taking A "True" Measurement

If you decide that your quilt would benefit from some type of border treatment, there is one very important construction tip to consider. Your quilt is much more likely to finish "square" and flat, with unrippled edges, if you coax the quilt to fit properly cut borders. In other words, before planning or cutting borders for your quilt, it is important that you know the "true" measurements of your top, so that the borders can be cut to match these measurements. What are these "true" measurements...and how can you find them on your quilt?

It is not at all uncommon for even the most carefully planned quilt to vary a bit in its dimensions. The length measured at the center, for example, may be different from the length at the edges. This variation may be due to miniscule deviations in cutting or piecing. Stretching along the outer edge may result from the simple act of

Figure 8-1
The "no border" option.

handling the top through the various stages of construction. Whatever the cause, this variation in measurement can spell disaster if you are not aware of it and prepared to deal with it.

When calculating border measurements for your quilt, be sure to measure through the center, rather than along the edges of your quilt (figure 8-2). This will result in the truest possible measurements. Plan and cut your borders to these "true" measurements, then pin and stitch the quilt to fit the borders...not vice versa! You may need to ease in a touch of fullness, but the end result – a nice, flat, "square" quilt – will be worth the effort.

Fewer Than Four Borders

Keep in mind that should you choose to include borders on your quilt, it is not necessary to use them on all four sides. Many quilts are very successful with only two – or even three – sides bordered. MIGRATION (see Chapter 2, page 31), based on an early nineteenth century crib quilt and TRIANGLES (Chapter 1, page 15), an actual nineteenth century bed cover, are good examples of the "fewer than four borders" option.

There are many possible reasons why some older quilts, including scrap quilts, are bordered on fewer than all four sides. Unlike today's quilts, many of which end up on walls or exhibited in shows, the vast majority of nineteenth century quilts were made for the bed, where often only three sides were visible. In the case of a scrap quilt, the whole cloth border, along with the backing, might represent the only fabric required to be purchased in quantity. A practical quiltmaker could conserve time, energy, fabric and expense by adding only those borders that were absolutely necessary. Then, of course, there is always the possibility that the *idea* of two or three borders simply appealed to the quiltmaker's sense of design – or independence. Whatever the motivation, however, you can follow the example of these innovators and experiment with this interesting border variation.

Plain (Whole Cloth) Borders

When it comes to placing a border on a scrap quilt, sometimes simple is best. I frequently rely on what I call a "plain" or "whole cloth" border to finish my quilt. Don't be

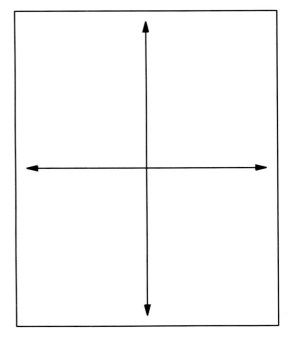

Figure 8-2
Taking a "true" measurement.

Figure 8-3

Plate 8-3
BEAR'S PAW, 94" x 100", Ruth McIver,
Johns Island, SC, 1984.
Flying Geese "circle" traditional Bear's Paw
(49-patch!) blocks. Viewer's Choice at
"Celebration of Quilts – 1985", Charleston, SC.
Collection of Mr. & Mrs. Herbert Todd McIver.

misled by the designation: plain simply means "unpieced." The plain border may be made up of fabric that is solid, print or striped, large scaled or small.

A plain border can help calm an otherwise "busy" quilt. Or, it can simply act as a frame, helping to contain the exuberant activity of many diverse fabrics. The quilt STAR LIGHT, STAR BRIGHT, shown in Chapter 2, page 29, demonstrates effective use of the plain or whole-cloth border.

Occasionally, a quiltmaker will use different fabrics for two or more sides of a quilt. This may be the result of running out and making do with what is on hand. It may also be a calculated design choice on the part of the quiltmaker. Whatever the reason, the results are often exciting...and fun. STARS OVER SILVER LAKE (plate 8-2, page 113) shows an example of a plain border that employs two different fabrics.

Another design possibility for plain borders is what I call the "pieced plain" variation (figure 8-3). In this variation, the plain border is pieced of two or three different fabrics, usually in random lengths. Whether resulting from necessity or thrift, as was sometimes the case in older quilts, or introduced as an intentional design element, the "pieced plain" border can add a sense of spontaneity to your scrap quilt.

Pieced Borders

Pieced borders are just as their name implies. Rather than a single length of fabric, these borders are composed of pieced blocks or units, chosen to complement, in pattern and scale, the body of the quilt. Simple squares, diamonds and triangles are frequently used to piece quilt borders, although more elaborate pieced designs are also used.

Pieced borders often work best when combined with restful plain or whole cloth borders which help to defuse potential busyness.

Both BEAR'S PAW (plate 8-3) by Ruth McIver and Nan Tournier's NIGHT SKY (plate 8-1, page 109) demonstrate mastery of the pieced border as a welcome component of scrap quilt design. Nan's bold pieced border is a fitting frame for her explosive multifabric medallion-style quilt. Ruth, on the other hand, has combined traditional Flying

Plate 8-2
STARS OVER SILVER LAKE, 40" x 40", by
the author, 1990-91. Two different fabrics
comprise the border of this wallhanging,
based on the traditional Ocracoke Island (NC)
Cracker block (four-patch).
The truth is...I ran out!!

Geese with a series of plain (solid and striped) borders to enhance her central design. You'll discover another wonderful surprise in the border of Ruth's quilt in the next chapter!

With careful pre-planning (use your graph paper here), corners can be designed to turn uniformly. Like many nineteenth century quiltmakers, however, you may choose to let your corners simply "happen." Select the option that feels right for the quilt – and the quiltmaker.

The Applique Alternative

Many applique lovers, convinced that scrap quilts are strictly for piecers, pass up the opportunity to experience the fun and the challenge of making a multifabric quilt. Yet many wonderful examples – from the last century and this – demonstrate that spectacular results can be achieved by combining the two techniques.

An appliqued border can make a wonderful frame for your scrap quilt. Darlene Christopherson has used many of the fabrics from her pieced stars to create the exquisite leafy vine that encircles her wall quilt EVENING STAR (plate 8-4, page 115). Kimberly Gibson has added touches of embroidery as well to the borders of INDIAN SUMMER (plate 8-5, page 116). In each case, thoughtful attention has been given to choosing an applique motif that suits the quilt in color, scale and design.

As with their pieced cousins, appliqued borders can be planned to turn with symmetry, or for a more unstructured, whimsical look, can be left to chance.

Combining Borders

Studying the photographs throughout this book, you probably have noticed that sometimes a combination of borders works best. A series of plain borders in varying widths, or any combination of plain, pieced and appliqued borders may be just the answer for your particular quilt.

Two important tools in planning the borders for your quilt are graph paper and your design wall. Experiment with a few graph paper sketches and use your design wall to try out a few fabric possibilities before making any final decisions.

A number of fine books cover, in detail, the simple

Plate 8-4
EVENING STAR, 40¼" x 40¼",
Darlene C. Christopherson, Sterling, VA, 1988.
Based on the traditional 16-patch block
(also called Variable Star), this small quilt
was a prize winner at the 1990 Leesburg (VA)
United Methodist Church show.

Plate 8-5
INDIAN SUMMER, 52½" x 52½",
Kimberly L. Gibson Charleston, SC, 1990-91.
The traditional Indian Hatchet block (four-patch)
is the basis for this wallhanging, a masterful
blend of piecing, applique and embroidery.
A prize winner at the Asheville (NC) Quilt Show,
1991.

math involved in planning pieced and appliqued borders. Check the bibliography, page 146, for resource information.

Squared vs. Mitered Corners

If you decide to border your quilt on at least three sides, the question arises as to how you will treat the corners where these borders meet. Depending upon the effect you wish to achieve, you may opt for either a squared or a mitered corner (figure 8-4). Either choice is perfectly acceptable; in fact, both the squared and the mitered corner are documented in nineteenth century quiltmaking. Neither option is more correct than the other. The key factors in making your decision should be which appeals to your eye and which best accomplishes the look you desire.

a.

b.

Figure 8-5
Attaching a "squared corner" border.

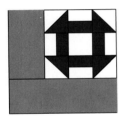

a.
SQUARED CORNER

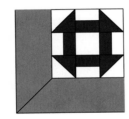

b.
MITERED CORNER

Figure 8-4

THE SQUARED CORNER

If you prefer a more humble look for your scrap quilt, you may want to utilize the squared corner to finish your border.

In this treatment, the corners meet at a 90-degree angle, as in STARS OVER SILVER LAKE (plate 8-2, page 113). To achieve this look, the two side borders are applied first. Next, the top and bottom borders are attached with a single straight seam (figure 8-5). In cases where a solid or subtly printed fabric is used, the junctures, when quilted, will be barely visible (plate 8-6).

The squared border treatment is effective for plain, pieced and appliqued borders – or any combination.

Plate 8-6
TURTLES, detail. Quilting helps disguise the seam where borders meet. A full view of this quilt appears in Chapter 2, page 28.

117

Plate 8-7
TROPICAL REEF, detail. The mitered corner emphasizes the "framing" effect of a quilt's border.

Figure 8-6

THE CORNER SQUARE

Another simple, but effective, way to finish a squared corner is with a corner square of contrasting fabric (figure 8-6). This corner treatment is most frequently associated with the traditional Amish quilt, but it can be just as effective for your scrap quilt as well.

THE MITERED CORNER

Many quiltmakers prefer the precise, ordered look of the mitered corner such as that shown in plate 8-7. In this corner treatment, the borders meet diagonally, at a perfect 45-degree angle. The effect is much like a picture frame, and indeed, this treatment bears consideration if the "frame" effect is what you seek. When a striped border fabric is used, mitering can yield especially interesting results (plate 8-8).

Mitered corners work well with plain and appliqued borders, as well as with any combination, and can be achieved simply by a variety of methods. Although I prefer to attach borders by machine, I usually complete the actual miter by hand, finding it the ideal means to a flat, perfect corner, free from puckers or bunching. Working by hand from the front side of the quilt also allows me additional control and accuracy when lining up striped or multiple borders.

Try this method for machine-attached borders with hand-mitered corners:

• Cut all borders. (I prefer to cut borders on the lengthwise grain of the fabric whenever possible). Side borders should be cut the true length of the quilt *plus*

Plate 8-8
LEFTOVERS, detail. Mitered corners on striped borders can yield interesting results.

two times the cut width of the border. Top and bottom borders should be cut the true width of the quilt *plus two times the cut width of the border* (figure 8-7).

Note: When I add multiple whole-cloth borders to a quilt, I usually join them together, treating the entire border as a "unit." All cutting measurements are based on this border unit.

- Mark the midpoint of each border. Then measure out from this midpoint and mark off the "true" measurement of the length or width of the quilt (figure 8-8).
- Generously pin the first border, matching midpoints as well as the "true" measurement guidelines with the quilt's outer edges. (Border will overhang equally). Ease slightly as necessary. Sew with the wrong side of the quilt facing you, stopping and starting with a backstitch ¼ inch from the edge of the quilt (figure 8-9). Press the border out from the center of the quilt.
- Pin and stitch the second border in like manner, being certain to keep the corner "flap" free (figure 8-10).

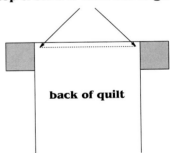

stop & start ¼" from raw edge

back of quilt

Figure 8-9

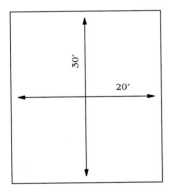

TO ADD 4" FINISHED BORDER
(Cut 4½")

Cut 2 borders: 20" + (2 x 4½")
     20" + 9"
     29" long by 4½" wide

Cut 2 borders: 30" + (2 x 4½")
     30" + 9"
     39" long by 4½" wide

Figure 8-7

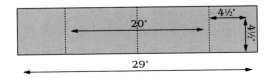

Figure 8-8

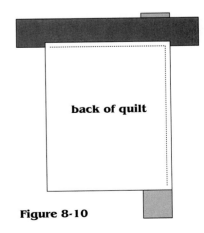

back of quilt

Figure 8-10

• Turn the quilt face up, smoothing out borders. Fold back one corner flap over the other to form a perfect 45-degree angle, using a right angle triangle to verify that the angle is exact (figure 8-11). Press and pin.

• Attach and pin-miter the final two borders.

• Select a thread that closely matches the color of the border fabric. Using a single strand, and sewing from the inner corner outward, "blind" or "applique" stitch the 45-degree seam (figure 8-12). If the border is a unit composed of different colored fabrics, you may need to switch thread colors to keep your stitches invisible.

• Press mitered seams open and reduce bulk by trimming to a ¼-inch seam (figure 8-13).

Some quiltmakers prefer to miter by machine. If this approach appeals to you, refer to the bibliography for assistance in tracking down the necessary resource information.

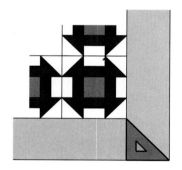

Figure 8-11

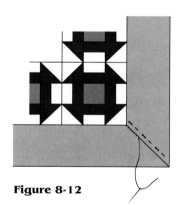

Figure 8-12

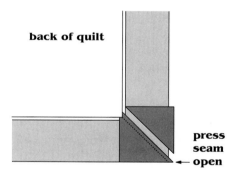

back of quilt

press
seam
← open

Figure 8-13

THE COMBINATION CORNER

When multiple borders are used, any combination of corner treatments can prove effective. In the case of BERYL'S CHALLENGE (plate 8-9, page 121), the narrow, innermost border turns the corner with a bright turquoise square. Two mitered borders of varying widths finish – and frame – the piece.

Remember...

However you choose to treat the borders of your scrap quilt:

• Select a border that complements, but does not overwhelm, your quilt. A scrap quilt, by the very nature of its many fabrics, generates a great deal of visual activity. You may want to treat your borders simply.

• Keep in mind the "look" or "feeling" you are trying to achieve. Appliqued borders with carefully planned corners are more formal and ordered. For a whimsical, "folk art" look, you might rely on serendipity!

• Use your graph paper and design wall as tools to preview possible choices.

• Base your borders on the true measurements of your quilt...not its edges. When pinning and sewing, coax the quilt to fit the border.

• There are no rules. Trust your eye and your instinct. Ultimately you know what works best for you and your quilt.

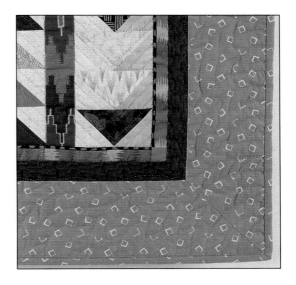

Plate 8-9
BERYL'S CHALLENGE, detail. Mary Underwood has used a variety of border and corner treatments in this quilt, which appears in the previous chapter, page 106.

CHAPTER 9
The Quilting Design

Plate 9-1
This photo of Ruth McIver's BEAR'S PAW reveals a delightful and playful surprise quilted into the border. The quilted "fowl" provide the perfect complement to her pieced Flying Geese border.

THE QUILTING DESIGN:
MAKING AND MARKING AN APPROPRIATE SELECTION

A thoughtfully chosen, beautifully executed quilting plan can do more than simply hold the three layers of a quilt together. It can add a wonderful third dimension of design, enhancing the pieced or appliqued image with additional depth and texture.

A quilting motif can convey an "attitude" as clearly as a particular color scheme, block design or set. Elaborate wreaths and vines are elegant and ethereal, whereas straight line or outline quilting can seem "homespun" and simple.

Whether you prefer to reinforce the angular geometrics of patchwork with strong, linear designs, or enjoy the contrast of feathers and curves, careful attention to the selection of a quilting plan can yield interesting – and often surprising – results.

Overall Quilting Designs: Traditional Options

Many of the scrap quilts of the nineteenth century are quilted in overall, sometimes called "utility," quilting designs. This choice of a single, overall motif seems logical for a quilt made up of so many diverse fabrics. The overall quilting pattern reinforces and supports the graphic statement being made by the quilt top; it does not attempt to compete with it. Marietta Briedenthal's WHEEL OF FORTUNE, detailed in plate 9-2, is an excellent example.

Some popular overall quilting designs of the last century (and the early part of this one) include:

GRID QUILTING

The simplest form of grid quilting is formed by intersecting horizontal and vertical rows of stitching (figure 9-1). Other forms of grid quilting include crosshatching and the Hanging Diamond pattern, which are described on the following page.

Plate 9-2
WHEEL OF FORTUNE, detail. The quilting motif creates a wonderful sense of movement in this quilt. See Chapter 6 for a full view.

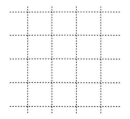

Figure 9-1
Grid quilting.

CROSSHATCHING

Crosshatching features an overall grid pattern of quilting formed by intersecting diagonal lines (figure 9-2). The resulting motif suggests "diamonds," which is an alternate name for this design.

The rows of stitching that form the crosshatched motif can be as close together as ¼ inch or as far apart as two inches, depending on the degree of texture desired. When deciding how fine crosshatched "diamonds" will ultimately be, consideration should be given to the overall size of the quilt, the scale of its individual blocks, the type of batting being used and the number of seams that will need to be crossed.

HANGING DIAMOND

A cousin to both the grid and the crosshatched motif, the Hanging Diamond pattern is formed by intersecting vertical lines of quilting with diagonal lines (figure 9-3).

PARALLEL OR DOUBLE PARALLEL LINES

Frequently stitched on the diagonal, this overall motif appears on many nineteenth century scrap quilts, especially those intended for utility purposes (figure 9-4). If the "homespun," traditional look appeals to you, you might want try this pattern. Quilting double rows adds textural richness to this simple design.

CLAMSHELL

Like its pieced counterpart, this motif draws its name from the clamshell it resembles in nature (figure 9-5). Its repeated curves provide a pleasant counterpoint to the geometric shapes inherent in many scrap block designs.

Plate 9-3
Darlene Christopherson has quilted diagonal double parallel lines over the surface of EVENING STAR, reinforcing the nineteenth century aura of her quilt. A full photo of this quilt appears in the previous chapter, page 115.

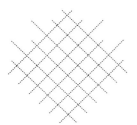

Figure 9-2
Crosshatching.

Figure 9-3
Hanging Diamond.

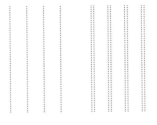

Figure 9-4
Parallel or double parallel lines.

Figure 9-5
Clamshell.

BAPTIST FAN

Baptist Fan is just one name for the family of overall patterns formed by quilting a series of concentric arcs – or quarter circles – to cover the entire surface of a quilt. (figure 9-6). No one knows for certain whether the name stems from its resemblance to the cardboard fans favored in the Baptist churches of the South or its popularity as the pattern of choice in many church-related quilting bees. More obvious are the names "rainbows" and "waves" and perhaps even "elbow quilting," so called because it followed the natural arm movement of the quilter as she rested her elbow on the frame.

Whatever name you choose to call it, the gentle curves of the Baptist Fan, like those of the Clamshell, balance nicely with the angular edges of many patchwork shapes. The motif is quite versatile, whether you prefer the traditional, or choose to adapt it to a more contemporary look as did Trish Gabriel in APPALACHIAN SPRING (plate 9-4, page 127).

Figure 9-6
Baptist Fan.

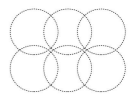

Figure 9-7
Teacup.

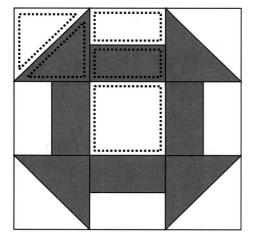

Figure 9-8
Outline quilting.

TEACUP

It is not difficult to imagine how this pattern got its name! A teacup, drinking glass or any other round household item can be used to form this overall surface design of interlocking circles (figure 9-7).

Alternatives

OUTLINE QUILTING

This popular method of quilting involves stitching or outlining each individual geometric shape in a pieced design, generally ¼ inch from the seam line (figure 9-8). Although not quite as popular in the nineteenth century,

Plate 9-4
APPALACHIAN SPRING, 37" x 53",
Patricia Mullins Gabriel, Conover, NC, 1990.
The overall quilting motif for this quilt is
a contemporary "take-off" on the traditional
Baptist Fan. The block is Water Wheel
(four-patch). Collection of Rosemary Gabriel.

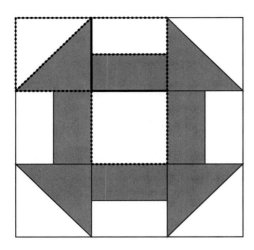

Figure 9-9
Quilting "in the ditch."

Plate 9-5
COUNTRY CROSSROADS, detail.

when overall quilting motifs were more common, outline quilting has become the preferred method for many twentieth century quiltmakers. It combines well when overall patterns are used in adjacent plain blocks, requires no marking (just a trained eye), and makes a fine choice if you like a clean, simple look.

QUILTING "IN THE DITCH"

Largely a twentieth century innovation, quilting "in the ditch" refers to the practice of outlining each shape in a pieced block by quilting directly along side or actually in the seam (figure 9-9). The quilt surface acquires some texture, but the stitching remains virtually invisible.

As a quiltmaker who loves the textured look and feel, as well as the beautiful drape, of a richly quilted surface, quilting "in the ditch" is my least favorite method of stitching. If, however, you are a relatively new or inexperienced quilter, whose stitches are still somewhat lacking in uniformity, if you are involved in a group project, where individual stitching may vary widely, if you are needling a particularly fat or difficult batt, or, if you simply like it, quilting "in the ditch" may be just the answer.

Filling The Open Spaces

So far, most of the quilting patterns that we have discussed have been rather simple – in fact, almost utilitarian – in design. This is very much in keeping with a great deal of the quilting found on the scrap quilts of the nineteenth century. Even when their quilts were set with alternate plain blocks, or contained lots of white space, nineteenth century quiltmakers relied on crosshatching, double lines and clamshells to fill these spaces as well. COUNTRY CROSSROADS, the nineteenth century scrap quilt shown in Chapter 1, page 13, is a good example. Notice how the quiltmaker chose double crosshatched stitching to fill the unpieced blocks (plate 9-5).

If, however, the quilting phase is your favorite part of quiltmaking, and you dearly love fancy baskets, wreaths and feathered designs, don't despair. Like you, some nineteenth century quiltmakers incorporated these well-loved motifs into the open areas of their quilts, often filling the background with crosshatching, clamshells or other overall designs. You might want to try this combination for a pleasing and authentic alternative. Consult the bibliography at the end of this book for some suggested quilt pattern sources.

Marking The Quilting Design

How to mark the quilting design on the quilt top is a question that continues to perplex quilters, despite the proliferation of marking tools on today's market. Perhaps it is the very scope of the choice that causes the confusion. Let's look at some of the possibilities.

A word of caution: before marking an entire quilt top with any marking device, it is wise to test it on scrap fabric to insure that the marking can be removed after quilting.

PENCIL

This old time tool is by far my personal marker of choice. Although not suitable for dark fabrics, I find it a dependable marker on most light and medium value fabrics.

Be sure to choose a hard lead pencil. I prefer the mechanical variety. Keep the pencil sharpened and mark as faintly as you can. Most properly marked pencil lines need no removal as the quilting stitch itself and the shadow it casts will cover any trace of marking. If, however, any pencil lines remain visible, they can sometimes be removed with a fabric eraser such as Magic Rub®.

Lack of satisfaction with this method tends to arise when the markings are made with a soft lead pencil or a pencil that has been allowed to dull. This results in a thick, dingy line that grays the thread and is difficult to remove. Remember: hard lead, sharp point and light hand!

WHITE CHARCOAL PENCIL

Artists have known about these for awhile. For a long time, the only place I could find them was in an art supply store; now they are available in quilt shops, through mail order and from vendors at various quilting events.

The white charcoal pencil is my favorite for use with dark fabrics, whether tracing around templates or marking quilting designs. The lead is hard enough to sharpen to a nice point, its markings are easy to see and seem to disappear when quilted. Unlike some of the wax–based pencils, it leaves no residue. As with a regular pencil, keep the point sharp and mark as faintly as you can.

Plate 9-6
Detail, INDIAN SUMMER (shown in full in the previous chapter, page 116). Delicate, feathery motifs can add richness and texture to the unpieced areas of your scrap quilt.

SILVER PENCILS

Once used primarily by architects for marking blueprints, these pencils are now widely available for quilters. In addition to silver, they also come in a variety of colors.

WASHABLE MARKERS

Now sold under a variety of brand names and in different colors (primarily blue), these markers claim to disappear when cold, clear water is applied. On the plus side, they are highly visible and very convenient when marking light and medium fabrics. On the minus side, they tend to dry out quickly.

In recent years, these markers have become somewhat controversial. Be sure to read the instructions carefully before using them on your quilt.

DISAPPEARING MARKERS

Similar to the washable markers described above, these "pens" differ in that their markings are designed to vanish automatically in anywhere from 24 to 48 hours. This can be an advantage to those who "mark as they go" or who don't want to worry about removal, but poses a disadvantage to those who prefer to mark the entire quilt top before basting or who live in humid climates where markings may not survive a sultry afternoon.

CHALK WHEELS

These markers took the quilt world by storm a few years ago. They come in a variety of colors (for marking light or dark fabrics) and draw neat, fine quilting lines that can be "brushed away" after quilting. The tiny chalk-dispensing wheel can be maneuvered through precut quilting stencils and is even refillable.

Be aware: some quilters report the lines can inadvertently be brushed away before they are quilted and there have been occasional reports that certain colored chalks can be difficult to remove.

SOAP SLIVERS, CORNSTARCH AND CINNAMON

No, that is not a grocery list! Many long-time quilters have used these time-honored, natural markers for years with great success. You might want to give them a try.

Marking: Before Or After Basting?

Many quilters prefer to mark the entire quilt top before basting, finding it easier to keep markings even, especially when marking straight lines. Other quiltmakers like to baste when the mood strikes them, even if they have not yet determined (or marked) the quilting designs for the entire top.

I have always been of the latter school; my quilts, including quilting designs, have developed rather spontaneously. A recent experience with crosshatching on an already basted top may, however, have converted me to the "mark before basting" method.

Selecting The Batting

This is a highly personal choice, based upon the quiltmaker's preference, the intended use of the quilt and the amount of quilting planned. I prefer the look and drape of the older quilt with its thin batting, softened by time. To achieve this look, try experimenting with the newer cotton battings or the 80% cotton / 20% polyester combination that has been popular with quilters for a number of years. Or, if polyester is your choice, consider the newer, lower-loft varieties available on the market today. Whatever your selection, be sure to read the instructions to determine if pre-treatment is necessary.

Check The Resources

My primary intention in this chapter has been to provide you with some guidance in selecting quilting motifs, particularly those most commonly found in nineteenth century scrap quilts. If you need specific information on the quilting stitch itself, please refer to the bibliography at the end of this book. It includes a number of excellent references that will prove most helpful in this regard.

Meantime, there are a few additional details to consider as you complete your "sensational scrap quilt." You'll find them covered in the next – and final – chapter.

CHAPTER 10
Final Touches

Plate 10-1
TROPICAL REEF, 23" x 23", by the author, 1990.
(Log Cabin/Straight Furrows set). Made for the
Great Art Auction, Watauga County, NC.
Collection of Shelton E. Wilder.

FINAL TOUCHES:
BACKING, BINDING, HANGING SLEEVE AND SIGNATURE

Little Things That Count

Even after you have completed the quilt top and selected and marked quilting motifs, a few important design decisions remain which can enhance the ultimate impact and appeal of your scrap quilt. The backing that you choose, the method in which you elect to bind or finish your quilt, the way you plan to add your signature – each of these decisions affords one last chance for creative expression. Why not take advantage of the opportunity to say something special about your quilt...and its maker?

Selecting A Backing

Many quilters prefer to back their quilt in muslin, determining it the optimum "canvas" for tiny, even quilting stitches and lots of elaborate quilting. While I admire this philosophy, I often feel that these quilters are cheating themselves of a wonderful last chance to have fun with their quiltmaking.

Choosing an appropriate backing for a scrap quilt can be as stimulating – and challenging – as composing the top. I love searching for precisely the right backing for a particular quilt, with *right* translating simply as *right for me!* While my normal fabric buying strategy is "half yards only...anything more stifles my creativity," I have been known to purchase anywhere from three to five yards of good backing fabric.

Frequently I find fantastic 100% cotton backing fabric on sale tables or in markdown bins. It is generally the only fabric I purchase with a specific purpose in mind, and I like to stock up. When I see a fabric I think might make an interesting backing, I buy it. There have even been occasions when I have designed the quilt to complement a particularly intriguing backing fabric!

What makes a backing fabric right for me? It may be a fabric that is the key to the design of the quilt top; but then again, it needn't appear in the top at all! While it often relates to the top in terms of color or theme (a blue-violet watery print backs TROPICAL REEF, page 133, for example), sometimes it provides a whimsical contrast instead. I once backed a sedate Amish-style wallhanging with a flamboyant length of tropical print...and called the quilt AMISH SURPRISE!

Interesting print backings are not at all unique to this decade...or even this century. Both TRIANGLES and OCEAN WAVES, pictured in Chapter 1, pages 15 and 21, were made in the second half of the nineteenth century. Each sports a wonderful print fabric as its backing (plates 10-2, 10-3), testimony to the individual quiltmaker's sense of design and adventure.

Backing may be whole cloth or seamed; composed of a single fabric or pieced from many. For additional interest, you may even choose to incorporate leftover, trial or "reject" blocks into the backing of your quilt. Keep in mind the "mood" or "feel" you wish to convey. Is your quilt simple and homespun? Elegant and refined? Dazzling and dramatic? Consider your quilt's unique personality as you choose the material and the means for backing it.

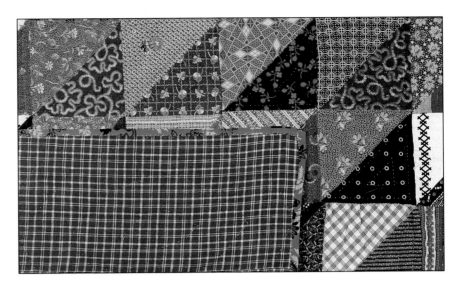

Plate 10-2
TRIANGLES, detail.

Binding The Quilt

Research indicates that the bias binding so highly regarded by quiltmakers today is primarily a twentieth century preference. While fabric does, indeed, tend to wear less easily on its bias edge, I prefer to follow a nineteenth century option and use a straight grain binding whenever possible, finding it generally easier to apply. I work with an older model sewing machine and do not have the advantage of a walking foot to help feed my quilt smoothly through the binding process. Binding cut to take advantage of lengthwise grain does not stretch, and my finished quilt lies and hangs "square" without the ripply edges quiltmakers dread. Since I make all of my bindings doublefold, they wear well too.

Just as in planning and cutting other elements of your scrap quilt, you needn't worry about running out of fabric for your binding. You can add a touch of spontaneity and whimsy to your quilt by piecing the binding, whether out of necessity or by intention.

Plate 10-3
OCEAN WAVES, detail.

Figure 10-1
Determining measurements for binding.

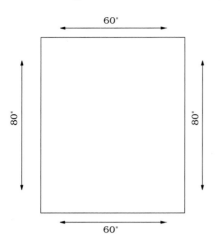

$80" + 60" + 80" + 60" = 280" + 12"$ (extra) = 292"
$292" \div 36" = 8.1$ or 8¼ **yards binding**

Figure 10-2
Pinning binding in place.

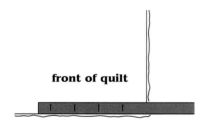

front of quilt

Ten Simple Steps For Straight Grain Binding

Making and applying a straight grain binding is amazingly simple. The ten-step process described below has been fieldtested many times by students in my beginner classes. Not only will you end up with a narrow, neatly applied binding, but with nicely mitered corners as well.

Read through the entire process once, then follow along, step-by-step. For best results, the entire quilt should be quilted before you begin to apply the binding.

1. Trim the excess backing and batting of your finished quilt so that it is even with the edges of the top.

2. To determine how much binding you will need, total the four outside measurements of your quilt. Add a little extra (12 inches or so) for turning corners and finishing. Divide this total measurement by 36 inches (one yard). This will tell you how many yards of binding you need (figure 10-1).

3. Using scissors or a rotary cutter, cut strips 2¼ inches wide by the length of the fabric. (You can cut your strips across the width if this method makes more economical use of the available fabric, but be aware that fabric cut on the crosswise grain will have a small amount of stretch.)

Figure 10-3
Turning a corner.

a.

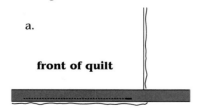

front of quilt

**Stop & backstitch ¼"
from edge.**

b.

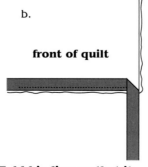

front of quilt

**Fold binding so that it
turns corner, forming a
45˚ (right) angle.**

c.

front of quilt

**Begin with a backstitch ¼"
from edge.**

4. Sew all strips (right sides together) so that they form one long, continuous 2¼ inch wide strip. Press seams open.

5. Fold raw edges of the strip together (right side out) and press to form a long, continuous 1⅛ inch wide doublefold strip. Wind around a piece of cardboard or a cardboard roll (paper towel type) to keep binding untangled. Press under a ¼ inch "hem" on the loose (starting) edge.

6. Starting in an inconspicuous spot (not a corner), begin to pin binding in place on the quilt, matching the raw edge of the binding with the raw edge of the quilt (figure 10-2, page 136). Do not allow a binding seam to fall on a corner; if this happens, repin. Figure 10-3, page 136, demonstrates how to turn a corner for a perfect miter.

7. Overlap your starting point by a few inches and trim excess binding.

8. Starting two inches past the overlap, sew binding in place, taking a ¼ inch seam. Stop ¼ inch from each corner, backstitch, flip the triangular flap and resume sewing (taking a backstitch as you start) ¼ inch from the corner on the next side. Continue around all four sides until you are almost at your starting point.

9. As you approach your starting point, unpin and trim the excess binding, allowing 1 or 1½ inches more than you'll need to finish. Tuck this "tail" into the starting end (figure 10-4). Since you have already pressed under a ¼ inch fold, this starting/finishing point will have a clean edge, resembling the other seams in your binding. Repin and continue sewing until you reach the point at which you started sewing.

10. Fold the binding over to the back side of the quilt and blind or hem stitch the binding in place (figure 10-5). The line of stitching from the front side will be your guide. Use thread that closely matches the color of your binding. Corners will miter neatly on the reverse. Using the same "invisible" stitch, stitch the corners – front and back – closed.

Figure 10-4
"Tucking" the binding.

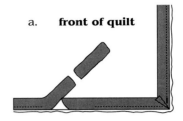

a.   **front of quilt**

Trim finishing edge of binding with excess of 1-1½"

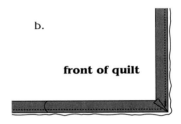

b.

front of quilt

Tuck raw edge of binding inside finished edge and complete seam.

Figure 10-5
Finishing with the "blindstitch."

back of quilt

Other Finishing Options

If straight grain binding does not suit your fancy – or your particular quilt – a wide variety of alternatives exist for finishing. In fact, entire books have been devoted to the subject! You'll find some of the various finishing options listed here, while the bibliography at the end of this book will direct you to a number of fine "how-to" resources.

BIAS BINDING

There are some instances when nothing else will do, especially in cases where you are dealing with a curved or scalloped edge. Many of the scrap quilts so closely associated with the 1920's and 1930's (for example, Dresden Plate and Double Wedding Ring) are often shown with curved edges. Perhaps this explains the popularity of bias binding in this century!

Bias binding differs from straight grain binding in that its strips are cut diagonally across the fabric as opposed to on the straight of grain. As mentioned earlier, bias binding tends to wear better than straight grain and it does have the advantage of stretching to take a curve. On the other hand, the very fact that it does stretch can render it difficult to handle. Extreme care must be taken while cutting and applying bias binding. It also requires more fabric than binding cut on the straight of grain.

Except in cases where a curved edge demands it, I find that the question of bias vs. straight binding is a matter of personal choice. Because I achieve better results, I am inclined to choose the latter.

ROLLOVER BINDINGS

If you look carefully at many older quilts, you will discover that they have no applied binding at all. Excess fabric from the back is simply rolled over to the front (or vice versa) and blindstitched in place to create a finished edge. TRIANGLES, pictured in plate 1-4, page 15, and detailed in plate 10-2, page 135, is a good example of this "rollover" technique.

A similar option involves turning excess fabric from the front and the back in upon itself and whipstitching the two together to form a finished edge.

If you hate the thought of making and applying a separate binding, and like the idea of carrying on a nineteenth century tradition, perhaps one of the rollover options will work for you.

PRAIRIE POINTS

Prairie points are constructed by folding squares of fabric into interlocking triangles for a sawtooth finish along the edge of a quilt (figure 10-6). Although not called prairie points until well into the twentieth century, the technique dates back to the mid-1800's.

What an enjoyable way to carry scraps right to the very edges of your quilt! WHEEL OF FORTUNE by Marietta Breidenthal (plate 10-4) demonstrates how effective this technique can be.

Signing Your Quilt

How much has been written in quilt publications over the past decade about the continuing effort to locate, identify and catalog our quilt history...and how much easier might the task have been had more women had the foresight to sign their work?

Who knows for certain why the vast majority of past quiltworks were left unsigned? We can speculate that quilting was "woman's work" and therefore insignificant and unworthy of identification, or that the very utilitarian nature of many quilts made signatures seem superfluous. What we do know now is that many quilts do survive, a testament to the artistry and skill of their makers and the sentimentality and reverence they arouse in their owners. It is worthwhile historically to recognize the origin of a quilt. It is also simply "nice to know."

We owe it to future generations to sign our quilts. While it may be easier in the future for quilt historians to document the quilts of the late twentieth (and early twenty-first!) century by the use of this or that manufacturer's line of fabric, a signature and date will assure the accurate documentation of our quilts and may even increase the pride and knowledge of our descendants who will be charged with the preservation of our handiwork.

There are many ways to sign and date your work. You may want to consider:

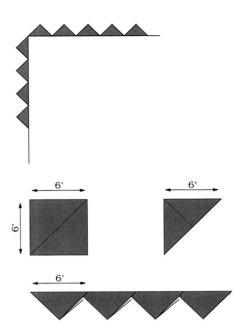

Figure 10-6
Prairie points.

Plate 10-4
WHEEL OF FORTUNE, detail. Many of the fabrics that appear in the quilt (shown in Chapter 6, page 93) are used for its prairie point edges.

Plate 10-5
APPALACHIAN SPRING, detail.

- Actually signing your quilt in quilting. Borders and sashes make good places to sign.

- Using embroidery on either the front or the back of your quilt.

- Cross stitching, either directly on the front or back of the quilt, using tear-away canvas as a basis for your stitches. Another alternative is to make a cross stitch label and affix it to the front or back of your quilt, as Trish Gabriel has done on APPALACHIAN SPRING (plate 10-5).

- Finding a spot in your quilt where a piece of cross stitch fabric can be substituted in a block (for example, the center of a Churn Dash or a blade in Grandmother's Fan) and actually incorporating your signature into the quilt. You'll need to plan ahead for this one!

- Attaching a muslin or other type fabric label. Pertinent information can be stitched, written (using a permanent marker such as a Pigma® pen) or typed on the label. If you choose the latter method, press the fabric to a piece of freezer paper. It will slide more easily into the typewriter.

- Carrying some design element from the front of the quilt to the back and using that to highlight your signature, as Kimberly Gibson has done with her quilt INDIAN SUMMER (plate 10-6, page 141). Perhaps you might applique a miniature block to the back of your quilt to be signed or used as a "pocket" for storing pertinent historical information. I frequently applique a large heart to the back of my baby quilts, indicating the names of the baby and its parents, and the date and place of its birth. Using a permanent marker, I add information about myself (name, hometown, date the quilt was completed) for further documentation.

You can be as straightforward or creative as you wish – I used a cutout fish as the label for my wallhanging TROPICAL REEF, shown plate 10-1, page 133. Use your imagination...but if nothing else, show your complete name, hometown and the date. Quilt historians, as well as future generations of your family – like those of Laura Chapman and Bunny Tassin (plate 10-7, page 141) – will thank you.

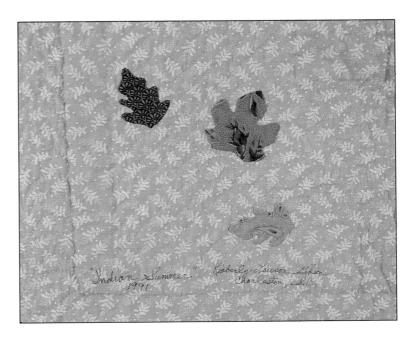

Plate 10-6
INDIAN SUMMER, detail. The quiltmaker has
signed her quilt with a permanent Pigma® pen.
Falling leaves echo the quilt's appliqued
border (see Chapter 8, page 116). Note the use
of print fabric for backing.

Plates 10-7
DADDY'S BOW TIES, details. This sentimental
quilt, seen in Chapter 6, page 81, is signed
and documented to commemorate a special
70th birthday.

Attaching A Sleeve For Display

Those of us who have been quilting and/or collecting for years know that eventually all beds are covered and another way must be found to display our favorite pieces. Many quilts, old and new, large and small, are moving to the walls as the focal points in rooms of traditional and contemporary design. In addition, countless quiltmakers are finding great satisfaction in working on small scale pieces. Limitations of time or simply the desire to try as many designs or patterns as possible makes the wallpiece an exciting option. Still others exhibit their quilts in shows and need to comply with show regulations regarding the preparation of quilts for display. Eventually, the dilemma of how to safely hang a quilt faces us all.

One of the simplest and safest ways to hang your completed scrap quilt is to affix a fabric sleeve to the back. If the quilt design allows, you may even attach two sleeves – one along the top and one on the bottom – so that the quilt may be turned periodically to mitigate strain and exposure to light.

Making a sleeve is simple...and definitely in the best interest of your finished quilted treasure. I generally use fabric left over from the backing of my quilt to construct the sleeve, although just about any fabric will do. Here's how:

- Using scissors or your rotary cutter, cut a strip of fabric 8½ inches wide by the finished width of your quilt minus a few inches. This strip can be cut either lengthwise or crosswise with the grain of the fabric. You may even piece it if necessary.

- Turn under approximately ¼ inch on each of the two narrow ends and topstitch with a thread that closely matches the fabric (figure 10-7).

- Fold in half lengthwise with wrong sides facing and stitch along the long edge, taking an approximate ¼ inch seam. This will form a long sleeve or tube, about four inches wide (figure 10-8).

- Press the sleeve so that the seam is centered facing you. There is no need to turn the sleeve inside out to hide the seam. It will be hidden when the sleeve is sewn to the quilt.

Finished width of quilt minus a few inches.

Figure 10-7

Figure 10-8

• Center the sleeve along the top edge of your quilt, just below the binding. Turn the seamed side so that it is facing the quilt. Using thread that closely matches the color of the sleeve, blind or hem stitch the sleeve to secure it in place along both its top and bottom edge (figure 10-9).

Figure 10-9
Stitching the hanging sleeve in place.

Why make your finished sleeve as wide as four inches? Most quilt shows and exhibits require a hanging sleeve, and four inches seems to be the size most often requested. Why not prepare your scrap quilt now so that you'll be ready when the time comes to share it proudly with the public. Even if you don't plan to exhibit your quilt, some future generation of your family just might!

A Final Word

Now you're finished! If this is your first time reading through this book, you are ready to roll up your sleeves and get started. A marvelous adventure awaits you.

If you have just placed the final stitches in your quilt, using this book as a guide, I feel certain that you have discovered that making a scrap quilt is an ongoing process. One seems naturally to lead to another...and another...

In either case, I wish you many, many "sensational scrap quilts."

BIBLIOGRAPHY/
Resource Reading

Plate 11-1
FRATERNAL TWIN II,
57" x 57", by the author, 1989-90.
Based on the traditional Friendship Star block
(nine-patch). Collection of Jason Brown.

BIBLIOGRAPHY/ RESOURCE READING

Bacon, Lenice Ingram. *American Patchwork Quilts*. New York: William Morrow & Company, Inc., 1973.

Benberry, Cuesta. "Charm Quilts Revisited: Part 1." *Quilter's Newsletter Magazine* (January 1988), pp. 30–31.

_____."Charm Quilts Revisited: Part 2." *Quilter's Newsletter Magazine* (February 1988), pp. 18–21.

Beyer, Jinny. *Patchwork Patterns*. McLean, Virginia: EPM Publishing, 1979.

_____. *The Quilter's Album of Blocks & Borders*. McLean, Virginia: EPM Publishing, 1980.

_____. *The Scrap Look: Designs, Fabrics, Colors and Piecing Techniques For Creating Multi-fabric Quilts*. McLean, Virginia: EPM Publications, 1985.

Binney III, Edwin and Binney-Winslow, Gail. *Homage to Amanda*. San Francisco: R K Press, 1984.

Brackman, Barbara. *Clues in the Calico: A Guide to Identifying and Dating Antique Quilts*. McLean, Virginia: EPM Publishing.

Bresenhan, Karoline Patterson and Puentes, Nancy O'Bryant. *Lone Stars: A Legacy of Texas Quilts, 1836–1936*. Austin, Texas: University of Texas Press, 1986.

Dietrich, Mimi. *Handmade Quilts*. Bothell, Washington: That Patchwork Place, Inc., 1990.

_____. *Happy Endings: Finishing the Edges of your Quilts*. Bothell, Washington: That Patchwork Place, Inc., 1987.

Finley, Ruth E. *Old Patchwork Quilts and the Women Who Made Them*. Philadelphia: J.B. Lippincott Company, 1929.

Fisher, Laura. *Quilts of Illusion*. Pittstown, New Jersey: Main Street Press, 1988.

Fox, Sandi. *Small Endearments: 19th Century Quilts for Children*. New York: Charles Scribner's Sons, 1985.

Hall, Carrie A.; and Kretsinger, Rose G. *The Romance of the Patchwork Quilt in America*. Caldwell, Idaho: The Caxton Printers, Ltd., 1935.

Holstein, Jonathan. "The American Block Quilt." *In the Heart of Pennsylvania: Symposium Papers*. (ed. Jeannette Lasansky). Lewisburg, Pennsylvania: Oral Traditions Project, 1986.

_____. *The Pieced Quilt: An American Design Tradition*. Boston: New York Graphic Society, 1973.

Horton, Roberta. *Calico and Beyond: The Use of Patterned Fabric in Quilts*. Lafayette, California: C & T Publishing, 1986.

_____. *Plaids & Stripes: The Use of Directional Fabric in Quilts*. Lafayette, California: C & T Publishing, 1990.

Hughes, Trudie. *Template-Free Quiltmaking*. Bothell, Washington: That Patchwork Place, Inc. 1986.

Johnson, Geraldine N. "More for Warmth than for Looks: Quilts of the Blue Ridge Mountains." *Pieced by Mother: Symposium Papers*. (ed. Jeannette Lasansky). Lewisburg, Pennsylvania: Oral Traditions Project, 1988.

Kentucky Quilt Project. *Kentucky Quilts 1800–1900*. Louisville, Kentucky: The Kentucky Quilt Project, Inc., 1982.

Lasansky, Jeannette. *In the Heart of Pennsylvania: 19th & 20th Century Quiltmaking Traditions*. Lewisburg, Pennsylvania: Oral Traditions Project, 1985.

Leone, Diane. *Fine Hand Quilting*. Los Altos, California: Leone Publications, 1986.

Martin, Judy. *Scraps, Blocks and Quilts*. Denver: Crosley-Griffith Publishing Company, Inc., 1990.

Martin, Nancy J. *Pieces of the Past*. Bothell, Washington: That Patchwork Place, Inc., 1986.

_____. *Threads of Time*. Bothell, Washington: That Patchwork Place, Inc., 1990.

McCloskey, Marsha. *Lessons in Machine Piecing*. Bothell, Washington: That Patchwork Place, Inc., 1990.

McClun, Diana and Nownes, Laura. *Quilts Galore! Quiltmaking Styles and Techniques*. San Francisco: The Quilt Digest Press, 1990.

_____. *Quilts! Quilts!! Quilts!!!: The Complete Guide to Quiltmaking*. San Francisco: The Quilt Digest Press, 1988.

McKelvey, Susan Richardson. *Color for Quilters*. Atlanta: A Yours Truly Publication, 1984. (out of print)

Orlofsky, Patsy and Myron. *Quilts in America*. New York: McGraw-Hill, 1974. (out of print)

Penders, Mary Coyne. *Color and Cloth: The Quiltmaker's Ultimate Workbook*. San Francisco: The Quilt Digest Press, 1989.

Ramsey, Bets and Waldvogel, Merikay. *The Quilts of Tennessee: Images of Domestic Life Prior to 1930*. Nashville, Tennessee: Rutledge Hill Press, 1986.

Rehmel, Judy. *The Quilt I. D. Book*. New York: Prentice Hall Press, 1986. (out of print)

Roberson, Ruth Haislip (ed.). *North Carolina Quilts*. Chapel Hill, North Carolina: University of North Carolina Press, 1988.

Simms, Ami. *How to Improve Your Quilting Stitch*. Flint, Michigan: Mallery Press, 1987.

Smith Lois. *Fun & Fancy Machine Quiltmaking*. Paducah, Kentucky: American Quilter's Society, 1989.

Thompson, Shirley. *The Finishing Touch*. Edmonds, Washington: Powell Publications, 1980.

_____. *It's not a Quilt until it's Quilted*. Edmonds, Washington: Powell Publications, 1984.

van der Hoof, Gail. "Various Aspects of Dating Quilts." *In the Heart of Pennsylvania: Symposium Papers*. (ed. Jeannette Lasansky). Lewisburg, Pennsylvania: Oral Traditions Project, 1986.

Wesbster, Marie. *Quilts, Their Story and How to Make Them*. Garden City, New York: Doubleday, Page and Company, 1935.

Wiebusch, Marguerite. *Feathers & Other Fancies: Quilting Patterns*. Kokomo, Indiana: Shearer Printing, 1982.

_____. *More Feathers & Other Fancies: Quilting Patterns*, Kokomo, Indiana: Shearer Printing, 1984.

ABOUT THE AUTHOR

Darra Duffy Williamson began quilting in 1982 as a result of long-time interest in American antique furnishings and artifacts. Teaching followed naturally – she holds a degree in liberal arts and education – and in 1989 she was named Quilt Teacher of the Year by *The Professional Quilter* magazine. She travels throughout the United States, lecturing and teaching for quilt groups and at seminars and symposia.

In addition to teaching, Darra exhibits her award-winning work both in competition and by invitation. Her free-lance articles, as well as her quilts, have appeared in a number of quilt publications and she is currently designing a series of original patterns for "Coming Home" of Carbondale, IL. A member of quilt organizations on the national and regional level, she is also active in the local art and quilt communities. She enjoys introducing children to quilts, particularly through the Very Special Arts programs in area schools.

Darra resides just outside the village of Blowing Rock, in the mountains of western North Carolina. She lives with her husband Bobby, who is also a quilter, their yellow and white cat, Buddy, and an ever-growing collection of antique quilts.

DARRA DUFFY WILLIAMSON

ᴥAmerican Quilter's Societyᴥ
dedicated to publishing books for today's quilters

The following AQS publications are currently available:

- **American Beauties: Rose & Tulip Quilts,** Gwen Marston & Joe Cunningham, #1907: AQS, 1988, 96 pages, softbound, $14.95
- **America's Pictorial Quilts,** Caron L. Mosey, #1662: AQS, 1985, 112 pages, hardbound, $19.95
- **Applique Designs: My Mother Taught Me to Sew,** Faye Anderson, #2121: AQS, 1990, 80 pages, softbound, $12.95
- **Arkansas Quilts: Arkansas Warmth,** Arkansas Quilter's Guild, Inc., #1908: AQS, 1987, 144 pages, hardbound, $24.95
- **The Art of Hand Applique,** Laura Lee Fritz, #2122: AQS, 1990, 80 pages, softbound, $14.95
- **...Ask Helen More About Quilting Designs,** Helen Squire, #2099: AQS, 1990, 54 pages, 17 x 11, spiral-bound, $14.95
- **Award-Winning Quilts & Their Makers: The Best of AQS Shows – 1985-1987,** edited by Victoria Faoro, #2207: AQS, 1991, 232 pages, soft bound, $19.95
- **Classic Basket Quilts,** Elizabeth Porter & Marianne Fons, #2208: AQS, 1991, 128 pages, softbound, $16.95
- **A Collection of Favorite Quilts,** Judy Florence, #2119 AQS, 1990, 136 pages, softbound, $18.95
- **Dear Helen, Can You Tell Me?...all about quilting designs,** Helen Squire, #1820: AQS, 1987, 56 pages, 17 x 11, spiral-bound, $12.95
- **Dyeing & Overdyeing of Cotton Fabrics,** Judy Mercer Tescher, #2030: AQS, 1990, 54 pages, softbound, $9.95
- **Flavor Quilts for Kids to Make: Complete Instructions for Teaching Children to Dye, Decorate & Sew Quilts,** Jennifer Amor #2356, AQS, 1991, 120 pages., softbound, $12.95
- **Fun & Fancy Machine Quiltmaking,** Lois Smith, #1982: AQS, 1989, 144 pages, softbound, $19.95
- **Gallery of American Quilts: 1849-1988,** #1938: AQS, 1988, 128 pages, softbound, $19.95
- **Gallery of American Quilts 1860-1989: Book II,** #2129: AQS, 1990, 128 pages, softbound, $19.95
- **The Grand Finale: A Quilter's Guide to Finishing Projects,** Linda Denner, #1924: AQS, 1988, 96 pages, softbound, $14.95
- **Heirloom Miniatures,** Tina M. Gravatt, #2097: AQS, 1990, 64 pages, softbound, $9.95
- **Home Study Course in Quiltmaking,** Jeannie M. Spears, #2031: AQS, 1990, 240 pages, softbound, $19.95
- **Infinite Stars,** Gayle Bong, #2283: AQS, 1992, 72 pages, softbound, $12.95
- **The Ins and Outs: Perfecting the Quilting Stitch,** Patricia J. Morris, #2120: AQS, 1990, 96 pages, softbound, $9.95
- **Irish Chain Quilts: A Workbook of Irish Chains & Related Patterns,** Joyce B. Peaden, #1906: AQS, 1988, 96 pages, softbound, $14.95
- **Marbling Fabrics for Quilts: A Guide for Learning & Teaching,** Kathy Fawcett & Carol Shoaf, #2206: AQS, 1991, 72 pages, softbound, $12.95
- **Missouri Heritage Quilts,** Bettina Havig, #1718: AQS, 1986, 104 pages, softbound, $14.95
- **Nancy Crow: Quilts and Influences,** Nancy Crow, #1981: AQS, 1990, 256 pages, hardcover, $29.95
- **No Dragons on My Quilt,** Jean Ray Laury with Ritva Laury & Lizabeth Laury, #2153: AQS, 1990, 52 pages, hardcover, $12.95
- **Oklahoma Heritage Quilts,** Oklahoma Quilt Heritage Project #2032: AQS, 1990, 144 pages, softbound, $19.95
- **Quiltmaker's Guide: Basics & Beyond,** Carol Doak, #2284: AQS, 1992, 208 pages, softbound $19.95
- **QUILTS: The Permanent Collection – MAQS,** #2257: AQS, 1991, 100 pages, 10 x 6½, softbound, $9.95
- **Scarlet Ribbons: American Indian Technique for Today's Quilters,** Helen Kelley, #1819: AQS, 1987, 104 pages, softbound, $15.95
- **Sets & Borders,** Gwen Marston & Joe Cunningham, #1821: AQS, 1987, 104 pages, softbound, $14.95
- **Somewhere in Between: Quilts and Quilters of Illinois,** Rita Barrow Barber, #1790: AQS, 1986, 78 pages, softbound, $14.95
- **Stenciled Quilts for Christmas,** Marie Monteith Sturmer, #2098: AQS, 1990, 104 pages, softbound, $14.95
- **Texas Quilts – Texas Treasures,** Texas Heritage Quilt Society, #1760: AQS, 1986, 160 pages, hardbound, $24.95
- **A Treasury of Quilting Designs,** Linda Goodmon Emery, #2029:·AQS, 1990, 80 pages, 14 x 11, spiral-bound, $14.95
- **Wonderful Wearables: A Celebration of Creative Clothing,** Virginia Avery, #2286: AQS, 1991, 168 pages, softbound, $24.95

These books can be found in local bookstores and quilt shops. If you are unable to locate a title in your area, you can order by mail from AQS, P.O. Box 3290, Paducah, KY 42002-3290. Please add $1 for the first book and 40¢ for each additional one to cover postage and handling.